YOU "SEE" WITH YOUR EYES!

An eye-opening look at a life and death experience, a trip to Hell and a trip to Heaven, while in a coma, that yielded awesome supernatural events in that life upon return.

SUE LAPRISE

To Marsha

You are

very precious

to The Lord! (Double)

New Blessings

for you!

Jim Japan

2022

You Shall "See" With Your Eyes!

Sue Laprise

ISBN: 978-0-9856424-0-2

You Shall 'See' With Your Eyes!

Published by: Sue Laprise Ministries
suelaprise@embarqmail.com

Printed and bound by TNO Bindery
Asheboro, North Carolina

Acknowledgments

To The Lord.

Many, O Lord my God, are the wonderful works
Which You have done, and your thoughts toward us;
No one can compare with You! If I should declare
And speak of them; they are too many to be numbered.
Psalm 40:5

To George, my husband.
A real man and modern day Noah, I love you!
Very impressive!
What a man!

To Jeff, my brother.
Thanks for everything! I express to you my deepest
Gratitude and thanks for being a brother that stuck closer
Than any brother would.
What an awesome brother you are!

To Judd, my cousin.
It is difficult to find the words that truly express
My gratitude.
Thank you for caring and going out of your way
To take me to a saving church
That loved the Lord.

CONTENTS

You Shall See With Your Eyes

FOREWORD

This book is simply amazing! Yes, it's an eye-opening look at a life and death experience, but it is so much more! 'You Shall See With Your Eyes' will encourage and inspire you like no other! I have no doubts whatsoever that whoever and wherever you are in your journey on this earth-no matter what you're facing or going through—this book will energize as well as ignite your God inspired hopes and dreams, and you too will be Victorious! It has blessed me beyond measure! In short, 'You Shall See With Your Eyes' is Miraculous! It clearly illustrates the fact that: With God ALL things are possible.

Larry D. Reid
Program & Music Director
WKXR Radio, Asheboro, NC.

INTRODUCTION

This book, **You Shall See With Your Eyes,** is an eye-opening look into a life that was dramatically changed. It is about a life and death experience, while in a coma, a trip to Hell, and a trip to Heaven, that yielded awesome supernatural events in that life upon return. The old life was filled with hopelessness, grief, sadness, and failure, resulting in life's circumstances, turning a churchgoer into an atheist. The new life, a wonderful life, a life filled with love, joy, peace, faith, hope, gladness, and yes, even singing. I was no longer an atheist, but a successful, victorious follower of Christ with a lot of confirmations, signs and wonders in my life. What wonders you may ask? The wonders Jesus talked about as I stood before him many years before laying in intensive care, "Sue, I will heal you, and these things will be a sign to the people, a confirmation that you have been to Hell and been to the door of Heaven and spoken with me. They would say that this experience was a vision, a dream due to the drugs they gave you to sustain and save your life, but because of the things I will do in your life, they will know, without doubt, that it has been a true life changing experience with signs, confirmation, evidence, and proof. This book, of supernatural evidence, is a display of the awesome working of the Holy Spirit in a life. Around 1982, the Lord gave me a prophecy, "They shall 'see' with their eyes the glory of the living God, and they shall not reason." This prophecy was immediately confirmed with the scripture, John 11:40, "Said I not unto thee that if thou wouldest believe, thou shouldest 'see' the glory of God?" This book is **that**! You shall indeed see with your eyes! You will see as you read this book that Jesus took my life from the position of profound difficulty, and by the Holy Spirit, turned it into a platform for the display of His Almighty power and grace.

Chapter 1

THICK DARKNESS

I was once an atheist, someone who did not believe in God. Thomas, one of the disciples, said, "Except I See...I will not believe" (John 20:25). I lay in intensive care, in a coma 4 days with only a respirator to keep me alive. The children I had held had died due to premature births and after several pregnancies I still had no children. Like Lazarus (John Chapter 11), I lay lifeless and powerless to do anything about my situation.

Prior to the coma, I began to hemorrhage seriously on a regular basis. I was known on my street for being picked up periodically by the ambulance. Just prior to this, I had told God I did not believe He existed, since He never seemed to answer my prayers. Due to life's experiences and the death of my children I determined He was no help. As a child I was brought up in church, I was what I call a churchgoer. I was there every Sunday, singing in the junior choir, attending youth group and all the other church activities. Then at a young age I experienced the funerals of my children, a lot of sadness and death. I told God I hated Him and if He did exist He was mean and I did not want anything to do with Him. I stared out the window that dark dreary night, my eyes fixed on the only light in my life at that time, a streetlight. I walked away from that place telling God I was done with Him from that day on and I was just going to live my life without Him.

Then suddenly, I found myself in intensive care. The police had informed my mom that I was not expected to make it. She watched as they tried to revive me. During that time I experienced something that has changed my life forever! I think at this point it is very important for people to keep in the forefront of their mind, as they read this account, that although I had been in church all the days of my youth, I had no knowledge or understanding of the Bible. Sermons and lessons were based on self-improvement, goodness, philosophy, etc. When I opened the Bible, it appeared to be written in another language. Yet, at this time, although I had no knowledge of scripture, the things I would experience would later be confirmed and verified by the Bible upon return. Keep in mind, at this time; I had never experienced anything supernatural, scriptural, or amazing. Most would have said, my life was sad, but normal; when you are living in darkness you get accustomed to it, you don't know anything different.

While in a coma, the first thing I became aware of was a falling sensation. If I could describe it, it was very similar to Alice in Wonderland falling and descending through darkness. The first feeling that I became aware of was overwhelming, oppressive fear. The second feeling I experienced was weight, or heaviness. Exodus 10:21,22 speaks of thick darkness, even darkness that may be felt! The darkness was so thick it had weight to it, like a heavy black velvet stage curtain, or theater curtain. Fear, panic and uncertainty gripped me as I stopped in mid air, still no bottom for my feet. Revelation 20:1 speaks of a place called the bottomless pit.

My hands pushed through the thick darkness only to find a room that was filled with caskets. The atmosphere was saturated with fear, evil, and death. A magician with black hair, in white face makeup, a tuxedo, a top hat, and thick black velvet cape stood before me. He tapped the caskets and instantly they all opened. The people in the caskets were dead but aware. The magician turned toward me and laughed. He proudly announced he could give life. As he tapped the caskets all the people sat up. They were stiff, controlled, and mechanical in motion, like a puppet or robot. As they sat up, they seemed in torment and pain as their dead bodies emitted a morbid tone and they groaned as if expelling air. The magician in a puffed up manner threw his head back with chilling laughter, mocking the dead that were under his control. Who was this magician? Ephesians 6:11,12 says, "Put on the whole armour of God, that ye may be able to stand against the **wiles of the** *devil*. For we wrestle not against flesh and blood, but against principalities, against powers, against *the rulers of the darkness,* of this world, against **spiritual wickedness in high places**." The magician was the devil. A shocking realization hit me as I continued to survey my surroundings; the place I was in looked like a funeral parlor, a place of death, I realized I was in Hell.

Memories of Halloween flooded my mind as I thought about the devil costumes and comical pictures of the devil I had seen as a child, never considering the devil or Hell to be real. How could this be? I stood in disbelief! I searched for a way to escape and saw none. As I looked into the faces of those around me, I saw misery and pain. The magician approached me boldly and pulled back a second black velvet curtain. Behind this curtain was an ornate golden altar. It was made of one solid piece of gold and gold animal heads adorned it. The horns of the altar protruded from ram heads and a golden goblet filled with blood was upon it. Hebrews 9:3 (NCV) "Behind the second curtain was a room called the Most Holy Place. In it was a golden altar for burning incense and the ark covered with gold that held the old agreement. Inside this ark was a golden jar of manna, Aaron's **rod** that once grew leaves and the stone tablets of the old agreement." Satan tries to copy God he is a counterfeiter. He stood with his magician's **rod** next to the altar. Exodus 7: 11,12 says, "Now the magicians of Egypt, they also did in like manner with their enchantments. For they cast down every man his **rod**."

Satan approached in a threatening way. He commanded me to drink from the blood-filled golden goblet. I refused. When I refused, he snarled, "Fall down and worship me." In desperation, I cried out, "Jesus, help me." Joel 2:32, Romans 10:13, Acts 2:21 says, "And it shall come to pass that whosoever shall call on the name of the Lord shall be delivered or saved." Jesus hears our voice in Hell! Psalm 139:8, "If I make my bed in Hell behold thou art there." And Jonah 2: 2 says, "I cried by reason of mine affliction unto the Lord, and he heard me; out of the belly of Hell cried I, and thou heardest my voice."

Suddenly, I heard the sweetest voice, a soft beautiful voice, say "Open the door." I looked around and could not see a door. Once again, I was engulfed by a thick, heavy darkness, as the magician took off his black velvet cape and whirled it over me. The darkness consumed me as his cloak of death filled the atmosphere. As I struggled to find a door I heard the sweet voice again, "Open *the* door." Then as if smoke was clearing I saw a door. I reached for the gold doorknob and as I touched it a harsh voice said, "If you pick the wrong door you will surely die." John 8:44 says, speaking of the devil, "He is a liar and the father of it." Fear and confusion seemed to stop me. As I hesitated and withdrew my hand, I heard the sound of three thunderous claps, as the single door became three doors. I knew at this moment I must open one of the doors to escape.

As soon as I overcame my fear and touched the doorknob, the three doors slammed together and became one. The three doors were an illusion; a trick to stop me, there was only one door. I opened the door and in the twinkling of an eye I was being hurled forward thorough darkness like a ball being hit by a bat faster than the speed of light. Then suddenly, I just stopped; I was just there, there in the darkness, as if in a cave, or grave. I cried, "I'm blind." 2 Corinthians 4:4, "In whom the god of this world (Satan) hath blinded the minds of them which believe not, that the light of the glorious gospel of

Christ, who is the image of God, should shine unto them." All I could *see* was thick darkness.

Chapter 2

GLORIOUS LIGHT

As I struggled to see, the darkness seemed to become even darker. Matthew 25:30 speaks of "outer darkness". Terror gripped me as the realization settled over me that I might never be able to see again. I looked harder, straining my eyes to see. Then suddenly, as my eyes searched the darkness, I saw a tiny white speck, it looked like a tiny piece of lint. My heart skipped a beat as I realized it was light. The dot of light began to grow into a crack of light, as if a door was ajar. My eyes stared intently as the light, like a sharp sword, penetrated and cut through the darkness. A door was opening toward me, as light continued to swirl and billow, pushing the darkness back and, finally, overtaking it like the waves of the ocean. My eyes beheld a splendor and dazzling brilliance words cannot describe. I beheld a face that beamed with love and eyes like flames of fire. The robe was more fluorescent and brilliant than any cloth; it was a robe of light. He was radiant and ablaze with Glory, to behold Him hurt my eyes. Like the sun, rays of light streamed from Him bathing me in love, kindness, goodness, peace, joy, reassurance, and gentleness, each beam of light having an attribute (Galatians 5:22). The beams of light that streamed from him bathed me in warmth, like the rays of the sun. His joy chased away the sadness, His light overtook the darkness, His love obliterated the fears, and His peace overcame the turmoil. There was power in His presence, His arms outstretched as if beckoning me. He was Love and His Love was Power. It was Jesus! There was no Peter or Paul at the entrance to Heaven, just Jesus!

He spoke, "I am The Door" (John 10:9). I looked at Him not understanding the things He said, clearly He was a man, not a door. "I am the Word." Revelation 19:13, "His name is called The Word of God." Once again I had no idea what He was talking about, He was a man not a word. "I am the true Light" (John 1: 9). I realized, at this moment, He was the Light, as I stood in the darkness. He continued, "And *the light shineth in darkness, and the darkness comprehended it not.*" He knew I could not understand Him or receive spiritual truths. I was, still, a natural man, and the Scriptures tell us that a natural man receives not the things of the Spirit of God; they are foolishness unto him (refer 1 Corinthians 2:14). It is true, I had been around spiritual things and gone to church every Sunday, but I had no spiritual understanding, I was like Nicodemus, the religious leader. Jesus said to Nicodemus, "Art thou a master of Israel, and knowest not these things?" (John 3:10).

Not realizing the enormity of the situation, I looked behind Jesus into Heaven; I saw beautiful lush trees, a wind-swept meadow and beautiful blue skies. I heard the lilt of children's laughter and the song of birds. It was an awesome place. I asked Him if I could get into Heaven. He said, "Truly, Truly, I say unto you except a man be born of the Spirit, He **cannot even See** the kingdom of God. For that which is born of the flesh is flesh, and that which is born of the Spirit is spirit. Except a man be born of the Spirit, *he cannot enter* into the kingdom of God. Marvel not that I say unto thee, ye must be Born Again" (refer John 3:3-12). Jesus did not ask about my denomination. He never asked about my religion, nor did He inquire about my goodness.

As I stood before the open door of Heaven, Jesus spoke again, "Behold, I have set before you an open door, which no one is able to shut. Behold in Heaven an open door, I have called you out of darkness, into marvelous light, no one comes to the Father except through me. I am the door, if any one enters by me, he will be saved. My words are trustworthy and true, all have sinned and fallen short of the glory of God, it is not of works lest any man boast." I continued to beg, I told him about the *good things I had done.* Then suddenly I was gripped by a feeling of shame. I looked down and to my surprise I looked like a beggar. I have always been complimented on my sense of style and dress. Now, somehow I was dressed in rags, filthy rags. Isaiah 64:6 says, "Our righteousness' are as filthy rags." I tried to hide the rags I wore but I could not. "You must Return!" His words pierced my heart. I cried and pleaded, begging Him not to send me back.

Then suddenly, before me was a beautiful gold mirror. Jesus said, "Behold, I will show you things to come." Jesus showed me many things that were hard for me to believe. Especially, the fact, that someday I would have children. He told me that my mission was to tell people about Hell and Heaven. To tell them that He was real and the devil was real, that Hell is a literal real place and that Heaven is real. He told me that some would not believe that I had been to Hell and Heaven. He said, "So the sign, to them, will be that you are healed and that you shall have children, something documented that you could not do. Also, when you return, you will understand the Bible, (Ephesians 4:18 speaks of your understanding being darkened); I have opened your eyes and turned you from darkness to light." This seemed like an impossible thing to me, a dream, and how could I ever have children? How would I understand the Bible? It all seemed so unreal. I did not understand all I heard, or all I saw, but I could clearly *see* the Light all around me, and Jesus before me.

Chapter 3

MARKED BY THE BLOOD

After this experience with the Lord, I did not know quite what to do with it. Although I now knew Jesus was real, my circumstances had not changed, babies dead, now divorced, intense inhalation therapy due to the respirator, I was still floundering, I had not yet gotten my sea legs. Finally, my cousin stepped in and led me to a church, and I began reading the Bible. My cousin and I, when we were little, had tried to read the

Bible, but it seemed like Chinese to us. Now, since my encounter with the Lord, the eyes of my understanding had been enlightened and I could understand every word. Moreover, I had become like David when he said in Psalms 119:99,100, "I have more understanding than the ancients." The Lord was giving me awesome revelation concerning the Word. The Word was lively to me, as if God was talking to me through it. The Word became very personal to me.

One night, my cousin invited me to his Bible Study and offered to pick me up. Before I left, I lay across my bed and read a few Bible verses. Noticing the time, I rushed to finish getting ready. I stood the bottle of cranberry nail polish on the new Bible my Dad had given me and carefully painted my nails. Suddenly, I heard a car horn; I jumped up and ran out to the car. Halfway through the Bible Study I decided to go downstairs to another class. As I moved down the stairs, I stopped, a strong presence was there, and I was riveted to the spot. My eyes darted about trying to take in the glowing light that seemed to be ablaze around me. (Acts 9:3, "Suddenly there shined around about him a light from

Heaven.") The light became brighter and brighter illuminating the room. Then suddenly, my attention was diverted to my Bible, I was horrified by what I saw. There were three bright red dots on the white pages of my beautiful new Bible. Regretfully, I went down the stairs, staring in disappointment at the three crimson spots. In frustration, I realized I must have spilt nail polish on the pages of my Bible. The disappointment would not diminish as I tried to overcome the feelings of sadness. I entered the classroom and soon forgot about the spots in the excitement of the lesson. Before I knew it class was over and the time had flown by.

As I was leaving, I glanced at my Bible…. The Red Spots were gone! I turned my Bible around and around studying all three sides, no red spots. I looked again, but the spots were not there. I rushed home; I examined my Bible more closely, only to find the pages bright and white. I lay across my bed to think: I knew, without doubt, I had seen those red dots; I had almost panicked when I saw them, and had become very sad, thinking I had ruined my new Bible with nail polish.

What happened? James 1:5 says, "If any man lack wisdom, let him ask of the Lord and He will give him liberally." I held my Bible close to me and prayed; holding it up, my Bible split and fell open to the book of Exodus. My eyes scanned the page and my heart raced as I read, "And the blood shall be to you for a token (or sign)....and when I see the blood I will pass over (or spare and protect) you" (Exodus 12:13). There it was the answer: God's beautiful gift; my Bible was marked by the blood. What a beautiful supernatural gift! What a beautiful sign! The truth was, I did *see* the blood!

Chapter 4

THE HOLY SPIRIT

I picked up my Bible to start my day with the Lord. I read the words the Lord gave me, but they did not mean anything to me. Again, I asked the Lord to speak to me, and again, the same words were before my eyes. Isaiah 55:1-3 "Ho, everyone that thirsteth, come ye to the waters, and he that hath no money; come ye buy, and eat; yea, come. Buy wine and milk without money and without price. Wherefore do ye spend money for that which is not bread? And your labour for that which satisfieth not? Hearken diligently unto me, and eat ye that which is good and let your soul delight itself in fatness. Incline your ear, and come unto me: hear, and your soul shall live; and I will make an everlasting covenant with you." Disappointed I put my Bible aside. I decided to listen to a new cassette series on The Holy Spirit. As I heard the speakers voice, it was hard to believe what I was hearing, "Ho, everyone that thirsts come to the waters, and he that hath no money, come buy and eat." It was Isaiah 55 the same thing the Lord had given to me 'twice' that morning. Joy and excitement swept over me, I shut the tape off and shrieked, "I am going to be filled with the Holy Spirit today!" My heart soared as I realized something awesome was about to happen. As I continued to listen to the speaker recite Isaiah 55 energy ran through my whole body. He explained that there is a difference between swimming in the water, and drinking the water. If you drink the water it is in you and influences you from the inside. If you swim in the water, the water is all around you and influences you from the outside.

I had, recently, been praying to be filled with the Holy Spirit with the evidence of speaking with tongues. The Bible tells us this is an important gift, and it is not a gift that has passed away. Acts 2:38,39 says, "Repent, and be baptized everyone of you in the name of Jesus Christ for the remission of sins, and ye shall receive the gift of the Holy Ghost. *For the promise is unto you, and to your children, and to all that are afar off."* I wanted the Holy Spirit to influence me from the inside and not just the outside. Jesus told the disciples that the Holy Spirit would dwell with them, and not only dwell with them, but be *in* them. John 14:17 says, "Even the Spirit of truth; whom the world cannot receive, because it *seeth* him not, neither knoweth him: but ye know him; for he *dwelleth with you, and shall be in you."* Then the speaker said, "You must choose to speak. God will give you the utterance, just start by saying, "Abba Father." I remembered Galatians 4:6, "And because ye are sons, God hath sent forth the Spirit of His Son into your hearts, crying, Abba Father." As I knelt in my room and repeated "Abba Father" I could feel the power and presence of God in the room.

Psalm 81:10 says, "Open thy mouth wide and I will fill it." Suddenly I could hear myself speaking a new language as the words Abba Father turned into a new language. At first I thought it was not real, (Satan tries to deny the gift because it is power) but as I continued I knew I had been filled with the Holy Spirit. Mark 16:16 says, "And these signs shall follow them that believe...they shall speak with new tongues." Joy filled my heart as I ran to my Bible and wrote the date, "Gift of tongues", April 19, 1981. The Lord is faithful and true; I did *see* the Holy Spirit come into my life with evidence,

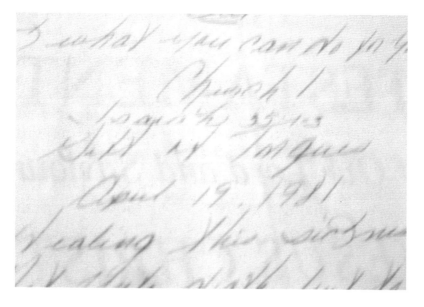

Chapter 5

A WORD OF KNOWLEDGE

One night, my pastor came for supper and began talking to me about his experiences in the Lord. He began to inquire about my life. As we continued to talk, I gathered enough courage to tell him about my Hell and Heaven experience. His eyes widened and he said, "I would like you to speak to the church Sunday night and give your testimony." That Sunday, the church was packed, especially, with teenagers. I gave my testimony not knowing what the reaction would be. As I closed, the teens stood to their feet with whistles, shouts, and applause. I had never experienced anything quite like it. The pastor gave an altar call and many people received Christ that night. That was a defining moment in my life. I could see God beginning to fulfill, in my life, the thing He had asked me to do. After the service, the pastor came to me and said, "Did you see all those teens respond to you? I have been having trouble getting someone to take the Teen Class on Sunday mornings; I think you should do it." Fear gripped me; I did not want to do it. I looked at the pastor and said, "Let me pray about it and I will get back to you."

The next morning, I was still amazed by what had happened the night before. Then I remembered my promise to the pastor, so I prayed, asking the Lord about teaching the teens. At that time I did not receive an answer, so I did not give it any more thought. That afternoon, the pastor called me and said, "I am just following up, have you received an answer?" I told him I had not, and did not feel teaching teens was for me. He continued, "Just keep praying, I know you hear from God, you will receive an answer!"

That night, the pastor asked if he could take me out for coffee. He told me about the impact the testimony had on some of the teens. He continued by telling me that only two teens had been attending the Teen Class and that was because their parents made them come, they did not want to be there. I finished my coffee and told him I still would have to hear from the Lord concerning the class. On my way home, I continued to pray about the Teen Class. Suddenly, something happened, a vision was before me, three large, brightly illuminated letters filled my mind: JFK. "JFK," I thought, "what is going on?" I continued to see before me the letters: JFK. Then I heard something within me say, "Remember what JFK said." So I started thinking, "What did JFK say?" I heard, "Ask not what your country can do for you, but what you can do for your country." "Yes, I thought, that's right, that's what he said." Then I heard, "Put **church** in that place." I quickly substituted church in the place of country. "Ask not what your church can do for you, but what you can do for your church!" I knew the Lord was referring to the Teen Class.

The next Sunday, the pastor never mentioned the Teen Class. He approached me and asked me to come to the Sunday night service, because they were going to have a special speaker. I told him that my husband and I had plans for the evening, and that I could not come. He continued, "I think you should come; I think that you will be blessed." That afternoon the Lord kept tugging on my heart concerning the Sunday night service. I told my husband that I felt I should go. Then my mom said, "Yes, I was planning to go, you can come with me." So, that night I went reluctantly to the service. As I listened to the speaker, my mind began to wander, I started thinking about the letters, JFK, I had seen. I had told no one about seeing the letters, or the vision, because it seemed strange to me. Suddenly in the midst of the service the speaker became very loud. With authority he said, **"Remember what JFK said, Ask not what your country can do for you, but what you can do for your country. Put church in that place"!** I almost fell out of my seat; I could not believe my ears. I ran up to my pastor after the service and said, "I'll teach the Teen Class." On the way home, I told my mom about the experience, the vision of letters, and how the speaker spoke the same thing that the Lord had given me. My mom looked straight at me and said, "That was a confirmation." The next Sunday I was teaching Sunday school.

Later, I learned that what I had received was a 'word of knowledge'. 1 Corinthians 12:6-8 says, "And there are diversities of operations, but it is the same God which worketh all in all. But the manifestation of the Spirit is given to every man to profit withal. For to one is given by the Spirit the word of wisdom; to another *the word of knowledge*." It was confirmed, I did **see** those 3 letters **JFK!**

Chapter 6

THIS SICKNESS IS NOT UNTO DEATH

The Teen Class was going great. It had gone from 2 teens to 50 in just one month. The teens were bringing their friends and family members. We could barely fit in the room. Shortly after taking the Teen Class, I became sick. My toes became swollen like little red balloons. Two weeks later, they became purple, bordering on black. I told some of the people at church and they took me aside, "You know what it is, don't you?" I answered, "No, I have no idea." They continued, "It's because you're doing such a great job with the teens. It's an attack from Satan." They introduced me to a lady in the church that had been healed of cancer. She began to tell me about her experience, how the Lord had given her a scripture, just before the doctors came in with a diagnosis of bone cancer. The Lord gave her Proverbs 3:8. It says, "It (the Word) shall be health to thy navel, and marrow to thy bones." She held on to that scripture for a year, while she battled the cancer. As she spoke, I thought of Proverbs 4:20-22, "My son, attend to my Words; incline thine ear unto my sayings, Let them not depart from thine eyes; Keep them in the midst of thine heart, For they are Life unto those that find them, and Health to all their flesh." Finally, her healing was completed. She was now healed.

As my condition worsened and my toes turned black and numbness set in, I went to the hospital. The doctor was very concerned and said, "Whatever it is, it is serious!" He thought it might be cancer or maybe something worse. The doctor x-rayed for bone cancer, and took tests for diabetes. So with more and more tests and no diagnosis, I went home feeling very sick and feeling like I was about to die. The doctor called and said my tests were negative. So my mom made an appointment with a doctor in Boston that afternoon.

I entered the doctor's office and immediately, the doctor knew what was wrong, I was diagnosed with Reynaud's Disease. He told me I would have to come to the office once a week for shots in my legs, and it would be something I would have to deal with for the rest of my life. As I thought about this on the way home, something within me could not accept this news. I lay on the bed with hardly any strength to lift my head. I prayed, "Lord help me, I feel like I am dying." I opened my Bible, suddenly I read, "This sickness is not unto death, but for the glory of God, that the Son of God might be glorified thereby." What an awesome word! At that moment, I heard the phone ring. My mom told me the lady that had been healed of cancer called. She had been praying for me and the Lord gave her a scripture concerning me. She wants you to look up John 11:4. I was amazed; it was the scripture I had just read.

That Sunday I was unable to go to church. The medication was causing terrible side effects. I now weighed about 98 pounds and this caused the condition to worsen. My aunt and several people who believed God could heal arrived at the house. We prayed together, and my toes were anointed with oil. The next Sunday, I was still very weak and unable to go to church, but I looked at my toes and realized they were pink and the swelling was leaving. My cousin received a Word during the prayer circle, "O men of little faith, why do you doubt, how long must I deal with you? Whatever you ask in prayer, you will receive, if you have faith. Her faith has made her whole. She is healed!"

The following Sunday, I walked into church claiming my healing. I walked down the aisle so weak, and feeling so sick, but so determined. I walked up to my pastor and said, "I am healed, I want you to tell the church, the Lord has healed me!" He did. After the church service, people came up to me and told me I did not look healed, I still looked very sick. My husband put his arms around me and picked me up carrying me out of the church. When I arrived at the house, a wave of sickness overtook me. I was so determined concerning my healing, I threw all the medication away and said, "If I am healed then I don't need this." For three days, I was extremely sick, so sick that blood vessels broke around my eyes, and bruising occurred on my face. I was so weak, I could hardly get up, **but** when I pulled back the blankets I saw ten healed toes.

I smiled and rejoiced during this time of sickness, my toes gave me great joy in the midst of the suffering. People would call and ask how I was doing; my answer, "There are a few symptoms trying to linger, but I am so happy, I am healed!" As the days went by I grew stronger and the symptoms dissipated. Weeks went by and there were a few relapses, but I never gave in to the temptation. Did you know Satan tempts us to receive sickness? Regardless of my circumstances, I was healed. Satan tried to tempt Jesus (The Son of God) but Jesus said, "It is written." It is written: That by his stripes I was healed. Jesus paid a high price for my healing. And when someone pays for something, they want you to have it. I had opened my present, torn off the wrapping paper, threw away the bow and was not returning the gift of healing; it was just what I wanted.

Seven months had passed since the Lord had touched me. I had almost forgotten I ever had Reynaud's disease. I was teaching Sunday school, and I had joined the choir. Many people watched as the months passed to see if I, really, was still healed. I delighted in wearing opened-toed shoes to church, so everyone could see my healed pink toes. I was healed, I saw God's healing power working in my life, and I would never be the same the gift of healing is true and it is real. With God comes truth, confirmation, manifestation, and evidence!

Satan's mission is to try and convince us that God's Word does not work. The fact was, I was sick, I had a disease, and those were the facts. Many people trust in facts, but I learned an important lesson during this time, facts are not truth. The truth was I was healed; the facts were I was sick. Truth is greater than facts. I could *see* that truth is greater, and that truth changes fact...It was all over my beautiful pink healed toes! Isaiah 52:7 says,

"How *beautiful* upon the mountains are the *feet* of him that bringeth good tidings, that publisheth peace; that bringeth good tidings of good, that publisheth salvation, that saith unto Zion, Thy God reigneth!"

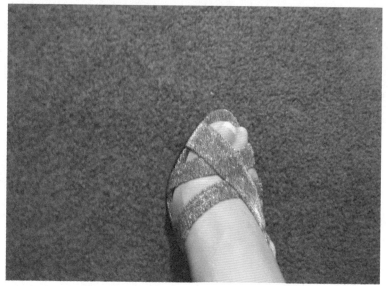

Chapter 7

SUGAR

As my husband and I worked on the house, my dog, Sugar, ran through the meadow, wagging her tail and keeping us company. Sugar always had a smiling face; she was my sweet, happy, fluffy white Samoyed. Sugar loved barbecues, and playing ball, digging holes to help us plant shrubs, and greeting everyone that stopped by. She really made you believe happiness is a Samoyed. Then, one day, Sugar became sick. This was a very sad day because the veterinarian could do nothing to help her. The Lord had a special purpose for Sugar's life, and I was about to find out what it was. Ecclesiastes 3:1,2 says, "To everything there is a season, and a time to every purpose under the Heaven: A time to be born, and a time to die." Sugar died.

In my sorrow, I needed to find out if Sugar was in Heaven. I asked my pastor. I asked my friends. I asked my mother. I asked my aunt. I even asked people who prayed a lot, but no one could give me any scripture. No one knew for sure. No one could help me. They tried to comfort me. They said they believed she was in Heaven, but these answers and speculations did not satisfy me or take the sorrow away.

James 1:5 tells us, If any of you lack wisdom, let him ask of God, and it shall be given. As tears fell, I prayed and a beautiful picture filled my mind. It was Jesus, smiling, and beside Him was a smiling Sugar (Sugar had lost her smile during her sickness). They were standing together in a meadow with other animals. Yet, even though this vision of happiness filled me with a supernatural joy and wiped out the sorrow, I still wanted solid evidence that Sugar was truly in Heaven. Once again, I thought about James 1:5, saying, "Lord, where is my answer?" Then, as quickly as the question was asked, the answer was given. I was reminded of Noah's ark: Genesis 7:14-15, "They, and **every beast** after his kind, and all the cattle after their kind, every creeping thing that creepeth upon the earth after his kind, and every fowl after his kind, every bird of every sort. And they went unto Noah into the **ark**, two and two." Then I was reminded of the manger: Luke 2:7,12 says, "And she brought forth her firstborn son, and wrapped him in swaddling clothes, and laid him in a **manger**...And this shall be a sign unto you; Ye shall find the babe wrapped in swaddling clothes, lying in a **manger**." I knew, without a doubt, from these scripture verses given to me that Sugar was in Heaven.

Amazingly, this is not the end of the story. Some time later, I was watching the boxer Sugar Ray Leonard, being interviewed by Howard Cosell. Sugar Ray had been injured in a fight and a detached retina was discovered. As he discussed his eye surgery, he told Howard that he had experienced something special, concerning his eye, after surgery. When the bandages were removed from his eye, his vision was halved momentarily: On the bottom he saw his family, and on the top he saw a *beautiful meadow with animals*, that he believed to be Heaven. My heart leapt within me, I jumped up and screamed, "Sugar is in Heaven!" The Lord had brought peace to Sugar Ray through a vision, concerning his eye, and through Sugar Ray's vision the Lord confirmed that Sugar, my dog, was indeed in Heaven. Amazingly, a man named Sugar saw a meadow, he believed to be Heaven, and it was filled with animals. I now knew my dog Sugar's purpose was to bring comfort and truth to little children and adults that have struggled with the loss of the pet they loved. I could *see* through this experience, the vision, the scriptures, and Sugar Ray's confirmation that, Yes, animals that we have loved do go to Heaven!

I would like to say here, that I have heard pastors on television state that animals are not in Heaven, yet, if we refer to the scriptures, Revelation 19:11,14 we are told Jesus is on a

white horse and the armies of Heaven are
upon white horses.

Chapter 8

DEMONS SPEAK

My life had changed in an extreme way upon return from my Heaven and Hell experience. I was acutely aware of spiritual things now, which was a vast difference from before. My life had radically changed, from a mere dreary existence, into a meaningful extraordinary life. I looked forward to waking up every morning. Life held a new excitement, something I had never experienced before. It was as if I had been awakened from a kind of walking death, my spirit, now revived, alive; the mere human existence and drudgery of life, overrun by fire and passion to meet every day with fervor. Each morning, I would grab my Bible and spring out of bed in order to hear from God. It was clear to me that my spirit, and my heart, had been touched and made alive by God. Now, not only did I understand the Word of God, but now, through His Word, He spoke to my heart. Notice the word heart has the word **hear** and **ear** in it. Our h*ear*ts are our spiritual ears, but only through the cross…**Hear**T. To me, the cross resembles telephone poles, and only through the cross 'T' are the lines of communication open to God. My heart could now hear from God.

As I read Psalm 103, "Bless the Lord, O my soul; and all that is within me, bless His holy name. Bless the Lord, O my soul, and **forget not all His benefits;** Who forgiveth all thine iniquities; **who healeth all thy diseases; Who redeemeth thy life from destruction** (or

Hell)." I began to recount His many recent gifts and blessings:

1. Deliverance from Hell

2. The blood on my Bible

3. Being filled with the Holy Spirit, with the evidence of tongues (Heavenly language, every kingdom has a language)

4. A word of knowledge (operating in the Spirit)

5. Healed from a disease

6. Receiving supernatural answers to unanswered questions (refer Sugar)

Needless to say, my new life was nothing like the old life, there was no denying the awesome change that had occurred in my life! Blessings were chasing me down and overtaking me, something that had never happened before.

One particular day, I was in the midst of a time of prayer and fasting. I was led, at this time, to pray and anoint myself with oil reading Ephesians 6:10-17. As I read out loud, "Put on the whole armour of God, that ye may be able to **stand against the wiles of the devil**. For we wrestle not against flesh and blood, but against principalities, against powers, **against the rulers of the darkness of this world, against spiritual wickedness in high places.** " I was amazed the Bible spoke of such things. I had been a churchgoer all my young life and had never heard these scriptures, nor heard this subject approached. As I continued, I imagined my loins girt about with truth and having on the breastplate of righteousness; my feet shod with the preparation of the gospel of peace; and taking the shield of faith, wherewith I am able to quench all the fiery darts of the wicked. Also, taking the helmet of salvation and the sword of the Spirit, which is the word of God. Reading the Word of God had become a supernatural experience to me, no longer dead and unappealing, but alive and piercing.

That night, I was looking forward to breaking the fast and going out to eat with my husband. Little did I know what was about to take place. As we entered the restaurant, we were greeted and escorted to a table between two other couples; one couple was in front of our booth and the other behind me. Suddenly, the light fixture over our table seemed to become much brighter and confusion seemed to ensue from the other tables. Loud cackling and chatter began at each table, my husband and I looked around only to notice just one person in each couple was participating, and the other person in each couple seemed confused and uncomfortable. My husband looked at me and asked, "What's going on?" I said, "I think it is demons speaking." Soon, they spoke clearly and loudly. "They're gambling in the **prayer house**...they're gambling in the **prayer house**." This was repeated over and over. I would like to interject here that many times demons incessantly repeat things. (refer Acts 16:16-18, "kept this up for many days.") Right away, I recognized the term 'prayer house' as a term, or phrase from biblical days, no one in modern day society calls the church a prayer house. Then I thought, "What does this mean?" Suddenly, I remembered the many 'Bingo' signs in front of the churches in our area. "That must be what they are referring to," I thought. Then each couple began arguing, asking, "What are you saying? What are you talking about?" Then, the person from each couple that spoke of gambling began interacting with the other. Those that were not participating in the mayhem asked, "Why are you talking to them?" "Do you know them?" They both told their partners, "No, I don't know them." Then the Lord spoke to my heart, "Familiar spirits!" I had recently read in 1 Samuel 28 concerning King Saul inquiring of a woman that had a familiar spirit (The medium of Endor), when the Lord would not answer him by dreams or the prophets of God. Leviticus 19:31 is clear, "Regard not them that have familiar spirits, neither seek after wizards, to be defiled by them: I am the Lord your God." We do not go to any other source for guidance or information; our Heavenly Father is the God of all wisdom and knowledge.

Then the spirits changed the subject from gambling to horoscopes, saying, "Yeah, I have got to check my horoscope to see if I am lucky. Yeah, I need to know if I am lucky." Then the other person spoke, "Yeah, I read my horoscope every day." I realized, I read the horoscope every day in the daily newspaper for fun. It wasn't something I took seriously or followed, but nevertheless, I looked forward to reading it as a form of entertainment. It was at that moment, I knew it was generated by the occult and more specifically Hell, and I knew from my experience that there is nothing entertaining about Hell, moreover, anything put out by Hell is always a hook, a snare, a trap. I made the decision right there, I was never reading another horoscope again!

I was amazed how spiritual things were being revealed to me, even on a day-to-day basis. These things being revealed to me, by God, had never been taught to me in church. I thought how successful Satan had been in covering all he does, and how, for the sake of popularity, churches have aided and abated him in keeping his works under his deceptive magicians cloak of darkness. We, as the church, should be crying out danger, danger, and revealing his evil, deceptive works.

Then, an excitement broke out between the two people, influenced by familiar spirits, "Oh, the holy day of obligation, the holy day of obligation!" Then the other, "Yes! the holy day of obligation. Tomorrow is our day!" I thought, "What is tomorrow?" Then I realized, It was Halloween. I had never heard it referred to as the holy day of obligation before. Still, I was aware that witches' balls and other Halloween Celebrations, in our area, took place on that day, honoring Satan. My husband spoke up, "I don't like this, let's go." So we left the restaurant. As I thought about what had happened, I realized the anointing of the Holy Spirit forced the demons to manifest themselves.

That night, we were having a bonfire in order to burn all the brush as a result of clearing our property. Some friends, that had helped us, were coming over to sit around the bonfire and talk. The guys put some kerosene on the huge brush pile and lit it. The brush burst into tall, deep orange flames. I could smell the crisp, spicy autumn air, as the snap and crackle of the fire seemed to fill my senses. The flames illuminated the deep, lush fiery colors of the leaves. Autumn had always been my favorite time of year. I decided to walk to the back of our two acres and check out our new foundation that had just been poured. As I looked over the foundation, my eyes were drawn to the beautiful autumn moon that shone above me, I began to pray and thank the Lord for all He had done. Suddenly, I felt led to walk around the foundation and anoint all four sides with oil, then I began to walk the borders and pray the protection Psalm, Psalm 91. As I walked the borders, I was aware of Heavenly angel activity, as if they were walking the borders with me. Psalm 91 says, "He shall give His angels charge over thee, to keep thee in all thy ways." I returned to the bonfire and I was enjoying the evening when suddenly the atmosphere got heavy. One of our friends was sitting in a lounge chair closer to the fire then I was; yet I was surrounded, once again, by extremely bright light, and again, I was aware of angels. Psalm 34:7, "The angel of the Lord encampeth round about them that fear Him and delivereth them." He was covered by a thick darkness; it was so thick I could no longer see his face. He had been drinking beer and had seemingly fallen asleep, but now all I could see was a silhouette in darkness, as his head seemed to be pulled up by a string, as if, he was a puppet. Then, he spoke in a growling tone, looking directly at me, "Do you want me to call Satan up out of this fire, I can you know?" I looked around as the light around me got brighter, feeling protected and safe, I said, "No, I do not want anything to do with Satan. He does not impress me, he has nothing I want." My husband interrupted, "What are you two talking about?" Our friend returned with a snarl, "She knows what I'm talking about! There are three kinds of people, those that have power from God, like her, and others like me that have power from Satan, then there are those stupid, miserable human souls that have no power and don't know what's going on, or why things are happening." Then He laughed in a way that cut into your soul, it was a wicked, evil laughter. I spoke up and said, "In the name of Jesus, Stop!" And with that, he sprung from the chair and picked up our picnic table, and with **super human strength** began to rip off the boards one by one and literally break them in pieces over his legs until the whole picnic table was destroyed. Yet, despite this display, I was not afraid. Mark 5:4 says, "**The chains** had been plucked asunder by him, and **the fetters broken in pieces; neither could any man tame him**," and Acts 19:14,16, "And there were seven sons of one Sceva, a Jew, and chief of the priests, which did so (exorcists). And **the man in whom the evil spirit was leaped on them (the 7 men), and overcame them, and prevailed against them, so that they fled out of that house naked and wounded.**"

As the bonfire died down, they poured more kerosene on the brush, the vapors of kerosene were so thick I could see them floating on the air. The scent of kerosene, seemed to assault my senses, it was all I could smell. I picked up my ginger ale bottle to take a drink. As I took two quick sips, it seemed as if the scent of kerosene was choking me. I put the bottle down and realized the distinct taste of kerosene was filling my throat and overtaking me. Someone had filled my ginger ale bottle with kerosene, using it as a container to pour kerosene on the fire. I rushed home and my mom called poison control, while she spoke to them, I prayed, all I could taste was kerosene! I opened my Bible, there it was, " They shall take up serpents; and **if they drink any deadly thing, it shall not hurt them!**" (Mark 16:18). My mom was very upset and said, "They say you need to go to the emergency room." I showed her the scripture the Lord had given me and went to sleep.

The next day, our friend came to our home and apologized for destroying our new picnic table, by saying, I am so sorry for ruining your picnic table I don't know what possessed me to do it. He did not know, but I did. He continued, "Also, it was me that used your ginger ale bottle for the kerosene." After he left, I thought about the day his mom had asked me to lunch, when I arrived she said, "I made an appointment with my fortune teller and I was going to bring you, but she called me and said not to bring you." Then another day he and his sister were playing a game and I sat down to play also, and they began yelling, "Go away! Go away! The board doesn't like you, your ruining it and making it upset." I felt rejected, so I asked, "What is the game?" "It's a Ouija board." God's hand of protection was on me even then, it's a wonderful thing when Hell wants nothing to do with you! Yes, it was as I had read earlier that day: "For we wrestle not against flesh and blood, but against principalities, against powers, against the rulers of the darkness of this world, against spiritual wickedness in high places."

I learned, and it was clear, Horoscopes, Ouija boards, Familiar spirits, Fortune-tellers all give messages, but they are not from the Lord and none of them are innocent or harmless. It was plain to see that the Lord was providing me with a window into the spiritual realm, on this side of things, and that deliverance (or casting out demons) would be something in my future. I could **see** I had experienced as

Jesus did and Paul did, demons speaking (refer Acts 16:16,17 & Mark 5:7).

Chapter 9

SINGING

My husband and I had just finished building our new, custom, one-bedroom house at the back of 2 acres. It had been a fun project and the house was beautiful. It had been a great season of smooth sailing. The only hitch was, toward the end of the project, the shutters I had stained and customized, for our kitchen bow window, bowed out and would not stay in place. This would be a costly mistake, if I could not work it out. I worked at the house most days from 7:00 am to 9:00 pm, but this particular day, I was discouraged and tired. I decided to leave early and go to my mom's. She was not at home, so as I waited, I cried to the Lord about the shutters and then finally, because I was so tired, I fell asleep. While I was asleep, I had a vision of my mom's kitchen cabinets, and in the vision I opened the cabinets, and saw a small magnet that clicked, and held the cabinet door tightly shut. I awoke and, immediately, ran to my mom's kitchen. I opened the cabinet and there, within the cabinets, were the magnets I had seen in the dream. I was so happy, realizing it was the answer to my problem. The next day, I purchased the magnets and installed them. The shutters were tight, aligned and beautiful, just as I had wanted them to be. Hebrews 4:16 tells us to come boldly to the throne to *get help* in times of need. I am so glad the Lord has the solutions to all our problems, no matter how big or how small.

I was now focused on my baptism. Jesus said, concerning His baptism, in Matthew 3:15, "Suffer it to be so now; for thus it becometh us to fulfill all righteousness." I had been sprinkled with water as a baby, but now, I was choosing to be immersed, as Jesus was. Although I had gone to Hell, and to the Door of Heaven and had an experience, I knew the real change took place the day I walked down the aisle of the church and, with a broken heart and tears streaming down my face, I gave my heart and life to the Lord. It seemed like that intense moment ignited my spirit and powered up my life. It definitely was the catalyst to spiritual gifts being made evident in my life. Still, there were promises Jesus had spoken to me that remained unfulfilled.

It had been many years since the Lord's promise of children had been spoken to me, and I had pushed the promise aside. Not only had I pushed it aside, but now I had built a custom *one*-bedroom home. In many ways, His promise still seemed impossible to me. Satan had painstakingly built a very formidable stronghold in my life of terrible pregnancies, hospitalizations, premature births, suffering and death. These very strong facts, that were repeated over and over, were the history of my life, a history I had lived through, suffered through and, in my mind, I had overcome and put behind me. Yet, as I journeyed with God through my life, I found that was not enough! God is an awesome God, and I do not use that word lightly. Truly, in my life and walk with God, I find Him to be a God of wonder. Be assured that getting over a defeat is not enough for God. Putting the failure behind you is not enough for God. The Lord tells us in Romans 8:37, we are *"more than conquerors,"* and He means what He says. God does not consider, just getting over it, or moving on, or putting it behind you and having great success in other areas of your life, as victory. The area we are more than conquerors in, is the battle zone. Where is the battle zone you may ask? It is the place in your life where you have failure, defeat, disappointment or loss, and the place you have left unguarded by moving on, thereby allowing Satan to trespass and set up camp. Satan lives in the stronghold of defeat, he lives in the stronghold of failure, he lives in the stronghold of disappointment and, most assuredly, he lives in the stronghold of loss. Satan sits up in that strongtower watching, waiting for a critical time, a more opportune time (refer Luke 4:13), to affect you in battle. Then, as he sees another battle approaching, as sure as tomorrow will follow today, he reaches out from that stronghold and takes you captive, leading you back to that place of defeat.

Shortly after the house was finished, I found out I was pregnant. I went to the doctor and he advised, that due to what he saw, and my terrible history, that I have an abortion. There was a law that permitted an abortion for the sake and life of the mother. So at the counsel of the doctor, I had an abortion. When I returned home, I felt the Lord had turned his face from me and forsaken me. I felt that old darkness, that old empty feeling in my gut. It was so frightening, I ran to my Bible only to read, "For a small moment, have I forsaken thee; but with great mercies will I gather thee. In a little wrath I hid my face from thee for a moment; but with everlasting kindness will I have mercy on thee, saith the Lord thy Redeemer. For this is as the waters of Noah unto me; for as I have sworn that the waters of Noah should no more go over the earth; so have I sworn that I would not be wroth with thee, nor rebuke thee. For the mountains shall depart, and the hills be removed; but **my kindness shall not**

depart from thee, neither shall the covenant of my peace be removed, saith the Lord that hath mercy on thee." I believed the healing, Jesus had promised, had not occurred yet, due to what the doctor was seeing. Satan had deceived me using the doctor's report and fear of facing death and complications again. I had made a dreadful mistake! Thank God for His kindness and His mercy! After I let the Lord know how sorry I was, I felt His loving arms surround me, but I knew from that point on to never do that again.

I would like to say here, as we discussed in the previous chapter, there are many voices and messages trying to influence our lives and decisions. Yet, even if a law says something is okay, even if the government says something is okay, even if a doctor says something is okay, or any other authority says something is okay, and the Lord says it is not, then it is not!!! More importantly, we know now, due to modern day technology, that a fully formed baby exists in the mother's womb nearly from the start. We know it is not a blob of tissue, or just some fleshy matter, it is, as pictures show, a precious human life. I am going to be blunt here, God says what He means and He is very clear, "Thou shalt not kill" (Exodus 20:13). I am blunt with you, because He was blunt with me. Satan is very subtle and cunning in plying his craft. But Jesus was clear, concerning him, and said, "The devil...he was a murderer from the beginning," (John 8:44). Jesus also tells us in this verse, "he is a liar, and the father of it." So two things Satan practices on a regular basis is killing and lying. Satan has been very successful in the area of abortion. People who would never participate in a murder or kill anyone, are now doing so through abortion. Think about this for a moment: We do not put people to sleep who are terminal and in extreme pain, why? That would be killing. We do put people in jail, who kill; no matter how heinously the person they killed treated them. Why? No matter what the reason, they have killed. Yet, an innocent baby, that has done nothing but sleep safely in its mother's womb, is ripped out of this protected place and killed. Before this, it was breathing, moving, living, it was alive. What can we say to the Living God, The Creator of life, concerning the killing of the precious and innocent? Typically, everyone sees a baby as a miracle; they see the handiwork of God at the moment of birth. The Lord says, "**Before** I formed thee in the belly I knew thee; and **before** thou camest forth out of the womb I sanctified thee," (Jeremiah 1:5). Babies are miracles that God intended to be protected, hidden away safely in their mother's womb.

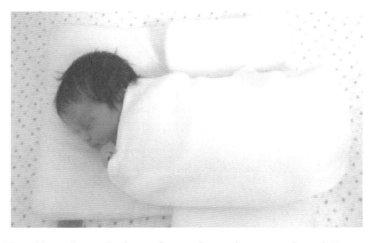

Finally, the night of my baptism arrived I was so excited. I stood in a beautiful white robe; I felt like an angel walking down into the pool, as my friend in his deep voice sang, "Now I belong to Jesus." My pastor immersed me, and when I came up out of the water, I felt an overwhelming feeling of being washed and clean. It was an awesome sensation that I will never forget. Yet, as I came up out of the water, my attention was drawn to a darkness above me, I saw *spirits like black birds or crows ascending and leaving.* What was I seeing in the spirit realm? I researched this and found that a flock of crows is referred to as a murder. I found out later, through deliverance sessions, with other women that had undergone an abortion, a spirit of murder would manifest itself. These women would cry when we would ask the spirit, "What is your name?" it would say, "murder," (Remember the restaurant in the previous chapter, spirits speaking, in public, through people) or they would see the word "murder" in their mind, or they would hear the word "murder." None of them wanted to say the word, they could not understand how they could have **'that spirit'** in their life, but the common thread was, they all had had an abortion. The Lord is a God of protection, He instructs us, in order to protect us (from depression and suicide), but He also respects our will and allows us to make our own decisions. Proverbs 26:2 tells us, "As the bird by wandering, as the swallow by flying, *so the curse causeless shall not come."*

A year or so had passed and I was writing, speaking at church, teaching, and ministering. Then, one night, I awoke to Is 54. It was repeated over and over again. My husband was sleeping and I did not want to disturb him, so I tried to ignore it and go back to sleep. Still, over and over, Is 54 was repeated in my heart and mind. I reached for a pen in the darkness, opening the nightstand draw, and finding a piece of paper I scrawled Is 54, and went back to sleep. That morning, I had coffee with my husband, kissed him good-bye, and proceeded to the bedroom, only to notice the piece of paper on the nightstand, I had totally forgotten about it. I sat on the edge of the bed and opened my Bible and turned to Isaiah 54. I could hardly believe what I read, **"Sing, O barren, thou that didst not bear**; break forth into singing, and cry aloud, thou that didst not travail with child." My heart jumped and my spirit leapt. I jumped around; I screamed, "I am going to have children. Oh, wow, I am going to have children." WOW!!!

That afternoon, my prayers were interrupted, by the sound like that of a radio; I heard music, beautiful music. I stopped praying and ran to the window, wondering, "Who was walking around our house, at the back of our 2 acres, with their radio on?" As I went from window to window, no one was there. I stopped to listen to the ethereal singing that filled the room. Then, as suddenly as it started, it stopped. This music, I had heard, was more beautiful than anything I had ever heard on Earth. I realized, at that moment, the beautiful singing was that of Heavenly angels, in confirmation of the given scripture, "Sing, O barren," and the prophecy of children. After this experience, it was clear that angels sing and praise God concerning a child being born on Earth. Luke 2:11,13 says, "For unto you is born…. And suddenly there was with the angel a multitude of the Heavenly host praising God!" Birth brings celebration in Heaven!!!

Thank God, God's ability to bless us is greater than Satan's ability to harm us. There is a moment in our life the finger of God points to the area of defeat and gently leads us back to that place of devastation, and by His love, His grace, His favor, His glory *He annihilates the defeat with overwhelming victory.* God knows these areas must be revisited by you and taken over by Him. Remember Moses, he ran away from Pharaoh's house, but *God sent him back*, not alone, and not without power. God through Moses showed Pharaoh who really had the power! 1 John 4:4 says, "Greater is He that is in you, than he that is in the world." That is why He tells us we are **more than** conquerors. What is a conqueror? It is one who masters, beats, defeats, overcomes, wins, succeeds, achieves, gains, overpowers, subdues, crushes! So if we are more than conquerors, then we will more than master the situation, more than beat it, more than defeat it, more than overcome it, more than win it, more than succeed, more than achieve, more than gain, more than overpower it, more than subdue it, more than crush it!

Let's reflect on some history. What was war about? Usually, gaining more territory. That is what Satan does, and he is successful at it in the lives of so many people. We as the church have settled for mediocrity, or just our little plot of land, fighting Satan just to keep that little piece. We have accepted status quo. Let me say, God is not a status quo God. Keep in mind; the battle **is** about gaining more territory. So what happens after the crushing, after the victory? The Lord tears down Satan's stronghold, and He builds something beautiful on the very spot Satan claimed. And that was exactly what the Lord was about to do in my life.

The months passed, then, one day, I realized I was expecting. I rejoiced again, but this time I did not go to a doctor. I had gone to doctors before, all to no avail. Everything seemed to be working this time, I looked great, I felt great, I was happy and all was very well. Then, out of concern, my sister-in-law called, she urged me to go to the doctor. I was six and a half months along and no problems. I reluctantly went to the doctor at her urging. Immediately, he sent for my records and told me my cervix was extremely thin and I would not carry to term. In fact, I needed to check into the hospital as soon as possible or I would not have the baby. When I came out of the office, my husband could see I was horrified. He asked what was wrong? I told him what the doctor had said. He replied, "I thought you told me, God said, you were going to have a baby. Do you want me to stay home with you?" "No, I told him, I am going home to pray, I will see what God says about it." He went to work and I prayed. I walked the floor and paced back and forth telling the Lord about the situation. I held up my Bible and said what do You say, Lord speak to me! My eyes fell on Jeremiah 17:5,7 it leapt off the page, "Thus saith the Lord; **Cursed be the man that trusteth in man, and maketh flesh his arm, and whose heart departeth from the Lord…. Blessed is the man that trusteth in the Lord, and whose hope the Lord is.**" (I would like to say at this point, I am in no way telling people what to do. This was God's word for me and my life. God can heal through doctors, and each person must seek the Lord for himself or herself). I decided not to return to the doctor. I stayed at home, happy, healthy, and expecting.

Finally, one day I counted the days, and months, realizing I was overdue. I prayed and asked God to direct me to the right doctor. I called and made an appointment. When I arrived, I told the doctor my story. He said, "I need to send for your records." I argued and said, "Please don't, every time the doctors see my history, I get bad news and they tell me I won't have a baby. He smiled and said, "Well, I don't think that will be a problem today. I see, from these tests, you are overdue, (something doctors said would never happen) and from what I can tell, beginning labor as we speak. You will probably have this baby sometime tonight." My daughter was born on Pearl Harbor Day (A day of battle). Something very strange occurred in the delivery room that day. The doctor held Georgia up and **proclaimed with a loud voice, "This is what Faith can do!"**

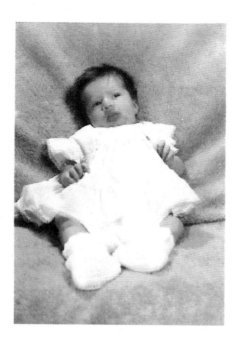

Georgia was born on 12/7 at 7:56 am, and weighed 7lbs, 12ozs. All 7's, God's fingerprint. The Lord had torn down Satan's stronghold and was building something beautiful in my life. I could *see* the handiwork of God in my arms.

Chapter 10

GOING UP

My daughter, Georgia, was now 4 months old and she needed a bedroom. As I mentioned in the pervious chapter, we had built a one-bedroom house. I called my cousin, an architect and man of God, he agreed to come to my home and pray. My brother, Jeff, and my cousin, Judd, arrived at 6:30 pm that night. We discussed some ideas and then went into prayer asking the Lord for direction concerning the house. During our prayer, we all saw a large flash of light streak like lightning across the bow window. Jeff and Judd said, "What was that?" I replied, "I don't know." We thought it was strange since the flash of light was so vivid and intense during our prayer. Later I found that the new light next to the door had blown out, popped, and shattered. Judd and Jeff were amazed; we were contemplating more construction since we had recently completed the new house. I shared with them Isaiah 54 and said, "The Lord says I will have, plural, *children*, so where will I put them?" Judd said, "Well, that rules out adding a room on." Jeff laughed, "That would be funny adding a room for every child, like a train one room after another."

I went to bed that night disappointed because I had not received any clear direction or plan. During our prayer, I did receive a word of knowledge, which was the name 'Roberts'. It turned out to be something concerning one of Judd's clients. Still, nothing concerning the direction we should take concerning the house. Prior to these events, I had prayed concerning the house and asked the Lord for direction. I was reading in the book of 2

Samuel, chapter 2, verse 1 about David and Hebron, still, nothing to guide me. That night I prayed and went to sleep; as I slept I saw in large letters **HEBRON.** I knew the word was referring to the scripture I had read the day before, still, I continued sleeping. Like every morning, I had coffee with my husband. He asked if we had received any direction concerning what we should do, I told him there was nothing at this point. I kissed him good-bye and proceeded to the bedroom. I picked up my Bible and started reading where I had left off the day before. My eyes were drawn to the words and David **enquired** of the Lord, I had been inquiring. "Lord," I said, "I have been inquiring like David and he got an answer immediately." My eyes fell on the word **Hebron**. My heart quickened! Hebron, I saw that word last night in a vision, what does that mean? Then I read, **Go Up!** The words, **Go Up** were illuminated in my mind.

Oh, Lord you want us to go up and put a second floor on the house? He reminded me of Isaiah 54, I turned to the scripture and read verse 2, "**Enlarge the place of thy tent**, and let them stretch forth the curtains of thine habitations, **Spare Not**, lengthen thy cords, and strengthen thy stakes." Certainly adding a second floor would be enlarging and sparing not! Wow, I could *see* the Lord had come with a precise and definite word, an exact plan.

26 I am distressed for thee, my brother Jonathan: very pleasant hast thou been unto me: 'thy love to me was wonderful, passing the love of women.
27 How are the mighty fallen, and the weapons of war perished!

CHAPTER 2

AND it came to pass after this, that David ᵃenquired of the LORD, saying, Shall I go up into any of the cities of Jûdah? And the LORD said unto him, Go up. And David said, Whither shall I go up? And he said, Unto ᵇHe-

b:31
Kin. 2:1

c Sam. 27:2

d h. 5:5

e Sam. 1:11

f s. 115:15

g Tim. 1:16

h Matt. 5:44

i Sam. 4:50

j Gen. 32:2

k osh. 18:25

Chapter 11

YES

My husband and I went to the bank and presented our plan. My friend, the president of the bank, said, "I believe the answer is going to be no. We do not do business like we did before, now we sell the mortgages. I would say, since things have changed, and you have recently completed a construction project on the same house, the bank will say, No." I could not believe what I heard. My husband asked, "What are we going to do?" I said, "This news is the same as the doctor's news. The Lord said we are having children and we did. The Lord said, go up, so we will." Several weeks had passed and as I prayed, my faith grew concerning His words, Go Up, Spare Not, Enlarge. Still, I asked the Lord about the bank's, "No." This is what He gave me, "Sue, you and I are a majority. It is done, the answer is Yes." Two days later the bank called the answer was yes, we could start construction with a closely monitored construction loan.

Within days, the materials, lumber, and windows were delivered. Things seemed like they were starting to go smoothly, after all, we had received a word from the Lord. Then the contractor called and said he had changed his mind he was backing out of the job. I told him all the materials were around the house, they had been delivered and we were ready to go. "Are you saying you won't do the job?" His reply, "No, I won't do the job. Sorry!"

We could not get another contractor on such short notice. So, I asked the Lord, "What are we going to do?" He gave me the scripture Exodus 31:3. So, I prayed the Spirit of all manner of workmanship would come upon my husband. My husband and brother took a few weeks of vacation, we assembled a crew, and my brother-in-law, who was a contractor, dropped by after his jobs. The shingles were stripped, the roof removed, the floor joists put in, decking put down, the walls were being raised and things were looking very good. Everything was on schedule and the weather had been great. Then, one night, we received news of a possible hurricane. My husband and the crew stapled thick, heavy plastic down, sealing everything they could. They removed the pump jacks and scaffolding from around the house to secure it from any damage.

I have to say here I have the greatest respect for my husband. Few men of God, even today, would have undertaken this immense project. I would say it was up there with Noah's ark. Truly, it was faith in action. My husband is an awesome man! Maybe you would say it is not such a big deal. For a little perspective watch the movie "Evan Almighty." Then, try to imagine taking your roof off and putting on a full second floor.

The hurricane hit with a fury and we did suffer major water damage. It was a disheartening time, a time of jeopardy. Everything was on the line.

Despite everything that was happening, the construction resumed, the roof was finished, the windows installed, and the house was enclosed. Still, with every forward advance, Satan was there to push us back. At this point, the enemy tried to pull the entire rug out from under us. The inside was not finished, the bank would not lend us any more money, and the insurance company was offering only $500 for water damage. I realized I was not just in a battle, Satan had declared war!

I hope you always remember this: Once we are armed with God's Word, His promise, His Yes, we are ready for battle. We have the shield of faith, wherewith we are able to quench all the fiery darts of the wicked one. For God's 'Yes' is a shield and it quenches every no, every fiery dart no matter how many are launched against us, no-no-no-no-no-no-no. When a no enters our heart, know without a doubt, it is Satan's fiery dart, but

God is an all-consuming fire, and he causes our heart to burn with the all-consuming fire of faith. God's fire ignited by His Word quenches every no. We cannot yield to the appearance of things no matter how bad it gets. Surely the arrows will fly by day, but every day we must stare at God's Yes! "Yes, I have spoken it, I will bring it to pass; I have purposed it, I will also do it," (Isaiah 46:11). God's 'Yes' must become our chariot to victory. God's 'Yes' must be the chariot of fire carrying us through the battle as the arrows and fiery darts (no-no-no-no-no-no-no-no-no) bombard His **'YES'!** For that one 'Yes' cancels every no, because it is God's 'YES'. **We must know, that not man, not circumstances, not banks, not contractors, not storms, not money, not insurance companies, or Satan, not even the world can stop God from fulfilling His plan.** Romans 8:31 asks, **"What shall we then say to these things?** If God be for us, who can be against us?" It does not matter if the whole world stands up in unison and shouts a resounding, "**NO!**" before us. You and God **are a majority and nothing can stop you, if you do not give up.** It was a fact we were in jeopardy, and in danger of losing everything, but if Jesus was asleep and not concerned that the boat was full and the storm was raging, then I could continue to trust his word that we would not sink in the middle of the project, and arrive safely on the other side.

Mark 2:4 says, "**They uncovered the roof** where he was: **and when they had broken it up,** they let down the bed wherein the sick of the palsy lay." Uncovering the roof, foolishness to the natural man, but for the man filled with the words God had spoken to him and led by the Spirit, a supernatural act! Moreover uncovering the roof was an act of faith; verse 5 tells us as a result, "Jesus *saw their faith*." Jesus would not be asking us, "Where is thy faith?" (Luke 8:25), and I did not ask him, "Carest thou not that we perish?" (Mark 4:38). I could *see* that even though the boat was full, and the storm was raging, we were still floating because He was with us.

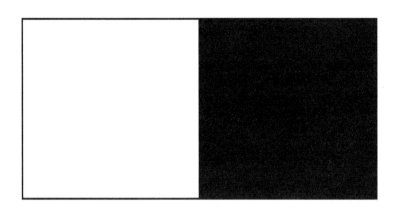

Chapter 12

A SIGN

Once I realized I was in a war, not a battle, I began to focus on one thing at a time. Satan is the god of distractions and confusion. I drew my battle line and concentrated on the insurance company. Some time had passed and we had received several offers, none of which covered the cost of the damage. I prayed asking the Lord to give me the 'exact' amount to settle for. "Lord, only you know, so please reveal it to me." After I prayed, my husband George got into the car and drove less than halfway around the city green (or rotary). Suddenly, I noticed a sign. What drew my attention was the fact it was a rectangle and half of the sign was darkness and half was light. My spirit was quickened, as the picture of that same rectangle of light and darkness was brought to mind. Some days earlier during a 3-day fast I had received a vision, and a word, in a dream. The vision: A rectangle, one half light, and the other half darkness. The word: I am light, accept what is in the light, it is from me; ignore the darkness! My heart leapt as I stared at the sign, it was identical to my vision.

In amazement, I read what was in the light...
"No Money Up To 22." I hit my husbands'
leg, "Honey, go around again I have got to
see this *sign* again."

As I opened the door to the apartment, I
realized I needed to know whether it was
2,200 or 22,000. "Please Lord show me." I
sat with my Bible, Nehemiah 7:71,72,
"Twenty thousand and 2 thousand...Twenty
thousand and two thousand." 1 Timothy 4:1
tells us "Now The Spirit speaketh expressly."
God is a specific God and He speaks specific
answers. The next day we took a picture of
the sign and put it on the refrigerator. The
Lord says in Proverbs 4:20, "Attend to My
words." I was paying attention.

The insurance battle went on, day after day,
week after week, month after month. I typed
letters to senators, the insurance commission,
and many others. I was relentless, mailing
out large envelopes full of pictures, estimates,
appraisals and other written material. The
battle raged on for well over a year as the
offers inched upward little by little. One day,
during the Passover season, I received a
scripture from the Lord, "If thou seest the

oppression of the poor, and violent perverting of judgment and justice in a province, marvel not at the matter (concerning the insurance company) for he that is higher than the highest regardeth; and there be higher than they"(Ecclesiastes 5:8). I knew that God was The Most High, His name is The Most High God and He was higher than they! This scripture led me to believe that the Lord was about to move on my behalf and put an end to the matter.

On May 7th we received a call from the insurance company; their offer was for 18,000. My husband was on the phone with them and they told him if we did not accept this offer, we would have to start the process all over again. My husband covered the phone, "Sue, let's settle, I don't want to go through this any more." I replied, " No! God said No Money up to 22,000. No! I won't settle." He told them, No, and hung up the phone. "Sue, I can't believe this; we should have settled." I repeated, "The Lord said, No money up to 22; 18,000 is not 22,000." I pointed to the picture of the sign showing **No Money up to 22**. As I finished my sentence, the phone rang; it was the insurance company, again. "We are tired of dealing with you, what do you want?" We replied, "We want 22, and it will be over." They replied, "Then just come to the lawyers office and pick up the check!" As I looked at the amount on the check and the picture of *the sign, No Money Up To 22,* I could *see* the faithfulness of God.

Chapter 13

BREAK FORTH

It is important at this point to stop and take account of everything going on so you can get a clear picture concerning the situation:

1. A new baby

2. A house under construction

3. A hurricane

4. Water damage

5. Moving to an apartment

6. Insurance battle

7. House not finished

8. No money from the bank

9. Husband gets a second job while doing his first job and finishing construction

10. Husband in a motorcycle accident

"And the rain descended, and the floods came, and the winds blew, and beat upon that house; and it fell *not*; for it was founded upon the Rock,"(Matthew 7:24). In the previous chapter, I mentioned that Satan was a god of confusion and distractions. Satan tries to shift our focus from the priority to the urgent. I could not afford to lose focus. Once the insurance battle was over, the next thing on the agenda was to finish what we started. After my husband had recovered, (he was totally healed by God), I returned to my unfinished home. The priority now was to finish the second floor interior. First the blue board went up, then the plasterers came in, the carpenters for the finish work, the flooring installed, and tiles were put in. The second floor was finally finished.

It was Thanksgiving, and we were definitely happy to be home and thankful that the enormous project was completed. The whole thing had been an amazing undertaking. Satan had come against us with tremendous opposition, trying over and over to stop the work. He had attacked us with distractions and he tried to create a lot of confusion. George and I were definitely like Nehemiah in Chapter 4 (refer verse 17 NCV). We carried burdens and worked at construction with one hand, and with the other hand held a weapon (the Bible). Verse 18 says, "Each builder wore his sword at his side as he worked."

That Thanksgiving of 1988, I told my husband I was expecting again. The Lord had told us through Isaiah 54 to **break forth** on the right hand and on the left, **enlarge, stretch, spare not.** That had all now been fulfilled. We had the Noah, Nehemiah, and Sarah experience all rolled into one. It had been an interesting and intense 3 years.

One day, my dishwasher broke, as insignificant as that may seem in light of everything that had happened, a broken dishwasher to a pregnant woman can be a big deal, in this case, it was the last straw. As I have found so many times, Satan always over plays his hand. Someone should have told Satan, " Do not touch a pregnant woman's dishwasher!"

The Sears man had come and the dishwasher could not be fixed, so I got ready to go to Sears in order to buy a new one. As I waited for George to come home, I looked around; we still had not dealt with fixing some of the things downstairs. The floors were worn from all the construction, the new hall stairway needed wallpaper, we needed plasterers to come to finish up and we needed furniture for the empty rooms upstairs. When George arrived, I told George about the broken dishwasher, "Sue, there is no more money for this project or anything else. We cannot go to Sears; you cannot get a new dishwasher. You are just going to have to pray to God about it, I can't do anymore. God started it; He will have to finish it." I totally understood where my husband was coming from.

The next morning, I stood in the kitchen; I looked at the broken dishwasher, the worn flooring and the water-stained ceiling. The water stain looked like a huge 'H'. After George left for work I lit into Satan with the word, "You are a liar. You cannot stop us. This house will be finished; it will be finished with the very best. You have fought us every step of the way but God said, we are having children and we are! And God said, go up and we did! He will finish what he starts. I will have new furniture not only that I will have all new appliances; I will have all new flooring. Everyone, including you, will see that God is great! The Lord gave me the scripture John 11:40 Satan! I believe and I will see the Glory of God. You think that 'H' stands for Hell and your signature in my home, but you are wrong. That 'H' stands for Heaven because the windows of Heaven are about to **break forth**. My God is limitless; He is a Spare Not God! He spared not His only Son will He not freely give me all things? The Lord told us to break forth and spare not and we did, now God is about to do the same." Just a week later I received a gift, tax free of $22,000. Everything I named furniture, appliances, flooring etc., I received and then some. The house was totally finished, and the last piece of wallpaper was put up the day before my second daughter was born. Rebekah was born on August 14, Victory Day (VJD). Like Georgia, Rebekah was also overdue. What a statement, what a Victory! It was a Day of Victory on all fronts. The Lord said, "Spare Not, Break Forth on the right hand and on the left." I could *see* His Word (Isaiah 54) was true and alive in my life.

Right hand   Left hand

Chapter 14

ELIJAH

It would seem with the fulfillment of Isaiah 54 in my life, the Lord's plan was complete, but this was not the case. In 1982, as I prayed about having children, after receiving Isaiah 54, the Lord also spoke of a son, Elijah. It was 1991 and I was getting close to 40 years old and if you are planning to have children close to that age, it makes doctors very nervous. The Lord had spoken to me about faith in action, so I had told people everywhere I spoke, that I was going to have a son, Elijah. As the years passed, some people asked, "Where is Elijah?" and some even seemed to mock, "I thought you were having Abraham, Isaac or whoever?" Still, I knew the Lord had spoken to me about a son. On the day of Rebekah's dedication to the Lord in 1989, I spoke and addressed some of these questions. "Today is a miraculous day for me, about 17 years ago, my first daughter, Rachel, died due to a premature birth. One year later a son died due to the same condition. Several pregnancies later, I was told I would never carry a child to term since my cervix worsened with each pregnancy, and finally, I was told I would never have children. Yet, today I stand before you a mother of two beautiful full-term, even overdue, healthy daughters. What has happened in my life? What is the difference between then and now? Just one thing...Jesus! Before, I made the decisions concerning my life, now I have given my life to the Lord. Matthew 16:25 says, 'Whosoever will save his life (or hold on to it for himself) shall lose it: and whosoever will lose his life (or give his life to the Lord) for my sake shall find it!' That is exactly what has happened to me, I have found the life the Lord meant for me to have and live.

There are people here today that 'know' my life has taken a 180-degree turn since I met the Lord. Yet still, you might wonder how all this came about: One night, in 1981 I awoke to what some might call their conscience voice, repeating over and over, Isaiah 54, Isaiah 54. I opened my Bible and read, 'Sing, O barren (a woman who cannot bring forth children), thou that didst not bear; break forth into singing, and cry aloud, thou that didst not travail with child, for more are the children of the desolate (or barren)…Enlarge the place of thy tent, and let them stretch forth the curtains of thine habitations: Spare Not! Lengthen thy cords, and thy stakes; For thou shalt break forth on the right hand and on the left.' Today, this scripture is fulfilled in your sight. We have children and our house is enlarged. Still, it was not easy; it took a lot of faith. It wasn't easy to be pregnant, remembering all that had happened to me in the past, and I don't know anyone in their right mind who would take their roof off. Now that takes faith! Yet, still, some of you might say, 'Yes Sue, but what about the other things that haven't happened yet? Such as the promise of Elijah?' *Yet*, is the key word, I stand in a long line with others from the Bible. Abraham waited 25 years for his son. I am no different than Abraham and those that have gone before me. Who am I to question God concerning His Word and His plan? If it had not been for the Lord, I would still be in Hell. I gave Him my life; I will wait with confidence just as Abraham did. More importantly, as everyone focuses on God's promise of Elijah, let us not miss the awesome miracles that have already been fulfilled in my life. I can only tell you, what God says, He will do!"

I spoke that message in 1989, and now, it was 1992. Ten years had passed since God's promise of a son. Then, one winter morning, in February, I decided to take the girls out for breakfast. We were so happy and just enjoying life. The girls were beautiful, healthy and smart and I was very blessed. As we laughed and talked during breakfast, a lady from our church stopped by our table, she greeted the girls and then looked me straight in the eye and said, "So, when is

Abraham, Isaac, or whatever his name, coming? I thought you said God told you were going to have son?" I was shocked. That evening I shut the door to my study and prayed, "Lord, I love you, but I think I may have been presumptuous. I really thought you spoke to me about a son. I am so sorry if I have made a mistake. Oh Lord, please speak to me." I sat down on the sofa, I opened my Bible and it is so hard to put in words the emotions I felt as I read this scripture, "And Rebekah had a brother!" Genesis 24:29. I screamed, I cried, I jumped up and down. Thank You, Thank You Lord, for answering me and confirming Your word, and Your promise. Immediately, peace flooded my entire being, I never questioned the birth of Elijah again. Some days later, I was coming down the stairway and, I know it seems strange but, in my spirit, I heard the little Dumbo song by Disney. I heard, *"Look out for Mr. Stork,* millionaires they get theirs," and then the song just stopped, *a month later I was expecting again.*

Everything was going great as I progressed in my pregnancy. That summer, we decided to go to a whaling museum during our vacation.

At the museum, they had a movie that talked about whaling of old and also about the Bethel. They said they would sometimes sit and wait for the move of the Spirit and someone might stand up and speak a message from God. They showed a clip: A man stood up in the Bethel pulpit, which was fashioned like the bow of a ship, and said, "Behold, a son is given." The baby leapt within me at the exact moment the man spoke. George saw my dress move, and asked, "Are you all right?" I was so excited, I stood up and said, "George this is it, this baby is Elijah"

On December 7, (Pearl Harbor Day) I arrived at the hospital in labor, and overdue again, (it is important to note here all births were natural). As a statement, or act of faith, the only clothes I brought for the baby were for a boy, specifically a white and green knit suit that had the words, "It's a Boy!" across the front. Elijah had come just as the Lord had promised and spoken. We called everyone and left the message, "Elijah has come," and then hung up. The first person we called was the lady from the church that had asked the question, "So when is Abraham, Isaac or whatever his name is, coming?"

Everyone could *see* without a doubt…"Rebekah had a brother!" Genesis24: 29

Chapter 15

JESUS IS LORD

During my pregnancy with Elijah, we received news of my husband's plant closing, the plant he had worked at for about 20 years. The pressure was really on, concerning the job situation. One day, after seeing the story in the Gazette, I cried as I drove down the long driveway to pick up Georgia from the bus. That day, the Lord touched me, and spoke to my heart, "If I care about you having a new van to pick your daughter up from the bus, certainly I care about your whole life." As I reached the end of the driveway, several doves (a sign of peace to me from the Lord) flew up before me, so many doves that it startled me. I never worried about the job situation again. Soon after those words from the Lord, George received a promotion, and began going to their North Carolina plant. George was gone two weeks at a time, two weeks with us, two weeks in North Carolina; this went on for over a year. It was not long after these events that he was offered a position with the company in North Carolina and we were asked to move. I told my husband that I would have to pray about it. It was hard to imagine putting our beautiful Garrison on the market, especially since it was a sort of 'museum of faith'. My mind went back, thinking about how far we had come and how much we had accomplished. It was amazing the transformation that had taken place. God had taken our one bedroom ranch and turned it into an awesome garrison. Even the name of the style of our house was amazing, a kind of recognition of the battle we had been in. A garrison, by definition, is a military post, a fortified place. I remembered the day I stood in the kitchen, praying in the spirit for more than an hour, and suddenly, a prophecy came forth, in a loud voice, I said, "They shall see with their eyes the glory of the living God and they shall not reason." I began to reflect on some of the comments: One of our friends that helped with construction repeatedly commented on the fact that it seemed like a church to him. Many that ascended the beautiful stairway, my husband had built, would stop midway to comment on the beauty of the sky reflecting through the glass doors and off the white tiles, it was as a stairway to Heaven. One December night, the driver that had picked us up from the airport and drove us to our home, literally gasped in awe, as I waited for my husband in the car. My husband had gone ahead to turn on the lights in the house. Suddenly, every window was bright and full of light, the triple glass sliders revealed the rich, red wine living room, filled with poinsettias, a fireplace, and candles, it looked like a Christmas greeting card. That night the streams of light, from the house, cascaded over the icicles and snow-laden trees. It was as if the glory of the Lord filled that place and the driver saw it. He gazed almost speechless and then said, "Wow, your house is so beautiful." This was the Lord's doing and it was marvelous in our eyes. In this house, I had experienced so many special things from the Lord. One precious gift was what I call the "Living Christmas Tree". The mirrored closet doors resembled a type of leaded glass as each mirror reflected the stately pines around the house. One day, a snow laden pine tree, outside my bedroom glass sliders, was reflected in the mirrors. My attention was drawn to the reds and blues vividly accented against the crystal white snow and the deep rich green of the pine. I redirected my focus to the window for a closer look, there nestled in the pine tree were many little creatures, blue jays, cardinals, nuthatches, chickadees, and plump, fluffy squirrels. The tree was filled to the brim and bustling with activity around the many bird feeders. It was a life-filled, beautiful, real Christmas tree, decorated by the Lord, Himself, how awesome, how extremely beautiful. "That must be how the idea of a Christmas tree came about," I thought. It was the most beautiful winter sight I had ever seen. James 1:17, "Every good gift and every perfect gift is from above, and cometh down from the Father." So many gifts, so many blessings!

Many people had come, to walk through this house, to see all the Lord had done over the years. Still, even before I received an answer concerning moving, I felt a strong leading to sell the house, and put the house on the market. Once again, I needed a sure word from the Lord. I prayed, "Lord, this is a very big decision, I must know your will. I need to be sure concerning this, I ask for a sign: If we are to move to North Carolina send something into the house that has the words 'Jesus is Lord' on it, then confirm it twice with 2 more things as confirmation."

One day, George came home and told me his company was sending us on a house-hunting trip. It had been several months since I had prayed about moving and still no sign, no answer. The company hoped that if we went out to eat, looked at some homes, and visited the area it would help us to make a decision one way or the other. Prior to flying out on the trip, I was told I would receive a house hunting package from the realtor we would be spending time with. Sure enough the large envelope came, I opened the envelope and poured out the booklets and papers. One booklet in particular fell open exactly in the middle where the staples were. I could hardly believe my eyes, there in large bold letters was the name of a real estate company Trollinger and across the two pages were written **JESUS IS LORD**.

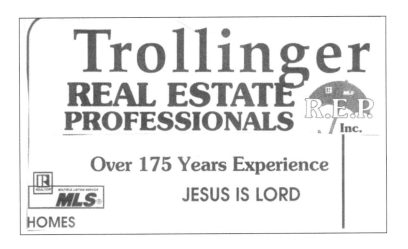

We were moving!

Century 21
Prime Site

Welcomes You To . . .

The trip to North Carolina was great. I went to an Assembly of God Church that Sunday and really enjoyed it. Still, I was concerned about the house we would buy. I prayed concerning the Lord leading us to the right house. That week, we made an offer on a house at a country club. Now all we could do was wait, I had put everything in the hands of the Lord. Psalms 37:23 says, "The steps of a righteous man are appointed."

Once I realized we were really moving, my focus shifted to the move and all that it would entail. I began praying about the movers, our furniture, our things, what our new house would be like. Once again, the Lord came with His great peace, and these were the scriptures He gave: Genesis 45:20, "Regard not your stuff; for the good of all the land...is yours." Also, in the Amplified Bible, Genesis 50:21, "Now therefore, do not be afraid. I will provide for and support you and your little ones, And he comforted them (imparting cheer, hope, strength) and spoke to their hearts (kindly)." When the purchase of the North Carolina home and the sale of our home did not come together, we realized the Lord must have a different plan. George continued to look for houses with the realtor; we had narrowed things down to only new homes. We needed a four bedroom and those were hard to come by. Again I prayed. Again the Lord answered with words written in red, "Peace be unto you....Why are ye troubled? And why do thoughts arise in your hearts?" That week, George sent me a new real estate book, as I looked through it, my eyes fell on a specific house, I called George and told him about it. He made an appointment with the realtor to see it.

That afternoon, when I returned home from shopping there was a signed agreement from our realtor on the table. I picked up the pen they had left on the paperwork. On the pen was the name of a Baptist church and in quotations the words "Jesus is Lord", again confirmation. That night, my mom came to visit the kids; she placed something on the table. She said, "I thought you would like this, it is a bumper sticker from my Bible Study, written on the bumper sticker were 3 words, "Jesus is Lord." I told her about the real estate book, the pen, and now the bumper sticker. Amazingly, after a second set of papers were signed, again on our kitchen table was a pen from another church with the words, **JESUS IS LORD!** I could **see** clearly the sign (the real estate booklet) and the confirmations (2 pens and a bumper sticker).

Chapter 16

I HAVE PREPARED

As I continued to pray about the house and the timing, concerning the move, I received a scripture from the Lord early one morning. It was Genesis 24:31, "Come in, thou blessed of the Lord; wherefore standest thou without? For **I have prepared the house and room.**" George called me concerning the house I had seen in the real estate booklet. He confirmed my feelings by saying, "I think this is the house. The only problem is that it is a three bedroom and we need a four bedroom." George continued, "But, I think it will work. Let me send you some pictures. I talked to the contractor and it could be perfect. He is still doing some finish work on the house and he said he would be willing to **add a room on to the house** and even a garage." I remembered the Lord's scripture that morning, I shrieked, "Honey, it is the house, go ahead and put a deposit on it". He was shocked, "What are you talking about you haven't even seen it. Wait, and I will send the pictures." I replied, "George, listen to the scripture the Lord gave me, '**I have prepared the house and the room**!' It's the house; I know it's the house! I know it sounds strange, but the Lord talks about taking care of the camels in this scripture, that would be our cars, the garage. I cannot believe this." Our real estate agent in North Carolina was shocked when my husband purchased the house. She said, "This is the first time in my 25 year career as a real estate agent that a wife has ever allowed her husband to buy a house sight unseen by her."

Our house had been on the market for a year, causing moments and feelings of frustration, but everything came together perfectly. The Lord had a plan, a house, an appointed time; *He really had prepared every single detail.* We were blessed to spend Christmas in our beautiful home one last time before we moved. The house sold in December and we were in North Carolina by January. As soon as I arrived, George took me to see the house the Lord had prepared, it was perfect. The Lord has taught me that He is a God of "Extreme Care" concerning His children. Also, I cannot speak more highly of the company and the move; we were treated like royalty. We had the best movers and Mayflower sent a special person to wrap our grandfather clock. The company provided a suite, while we customized our new house, and added on a room and garage. We ate at any restaurant we wanted, 3 times a day for 6 weeks. It was amazing! Ecclesiastes 3:11 says, "God hath made everything beautiful in His time."

The next few weeks were exciting as construction was going on, and we were moving in, setting everything in order. I am so thankful to the Lord, concerning the way everything was handled. It was so nice going back to the suite after a full day of organized chaos with the construction crew, the flooring people, the landscaping crew, the kids, a baby, and everything else going on. It was exciting, a lot of work, and a lot of fun! James 1:17 says, "Every good gift and every perfect gift is from above, and cometh down from the Father of lights." God is a good God; He is so good. As I look back, it is no wonder that the Lord said, "Come in, thou blessed of the Lord," and then asked, "Wherefore standest thou without? For I have prepared!" I could **see** that the Lord had clearly prepared the house, a room, a garage and so much more!

Chapter 17

THE WAR IS OVER

Before we knew it, vacation time had arrived and George began taking us to various places in North Carolina so we could get acquainted with where we lived. One day he planned a day trip to Greensboro and one of the sites on his itinerary was the Greensboro Museum of History. I really believe there are times the Lord likes to surprise us and bring wonder into our lives just to let us know that He is there. This day would be one of those days.

As you know from reading this book, I have had many profound moments in my life. Yet, if I were made to choose the one that had the most impact and awe it is this day that I am about to share with you. This was a day the Lord made the pieces fit like an enormous puzzle, and it would be this day that He would put the pieces of my life together and set the beautiful picture He had created before my eyes. It was *the* day I would see the big picture, concerning all the Lord had done. This was one of those indescribable days, a day of wonder, and a day that the Lord would call a marvelous day!

We arrived at the Greensboro Museum of History, I walked through the door, and it seemed like many of the other museums we had gone to, I did not see anything out of the ordinary. As I continued through the museum, I went up the stairs, I continued through a dimly lit area and saw a doorway ahead. As I entered the room, I could see newspapers lined up on the wall. I stood in the doorway, I just stopped, my eyes scanned the room, I stood in awe, and there before me were these headlines on broadsheets: **The War Is Over! Peace At Last! Victory!**

As I passed through the doorway these words filled my eyes, **The War Is Over! Peace At Last! Victory!** The big, black, bold letters surrounded me; it was an experience that is very hard to put into words. The moment was like an exclamation point in my life. I felt the presence of the Lord invade the room as I tried to process what was happening to me. I wanted to cry, I was filled with joy, and I was overwhelmed and amazed. These headlines were from World War II, so you may ask, "What did that have to do with you? Why were you affected by these headlines, these words?" As I continued to scan the walls I could hardly focus due to the emotions I was experiencing, I saw the most gripping sight, not only was I surrounded by words of Victory and Peace but **I was SURROUNDED by the DATES of MY CHILDREN'S BIRTHS!** Georgia was born on December 7, Pearl Harbor Day, Rebekah was born on August 14, Victory Day (VJD), Elijah was born on December 7, Pearl Harbor Day! Revelation 1:8 says, "I am Alpha and Omega, the beginning and the ending, saith the Lord." What He had started in my life He had finished. Isaiah 54 had been completely fulfilled, the children, that were impossible to have, the stretching forth, the enlarging of the house, everything He had promised He had accomplished. When there was no way He was *The Way* in my life. He had prepared everything concerning our move to North Carolina; maybe this was why I had moved to North Carolina, just to see His huge display of Victory in my life on the walls of the North Carolina, Greensboro Museum of History.

As I continued to stand in that room, I saw before me the annihilation of Satan's defeat in my life and the overwhelming Victory from the Lord. As I stood surrounded by His Glory, it was an awesome moment no one could comprehend. As I exited the room the Lord spoke to my heart, "Sue, in this life you will have battles just as your children's birth dates depict, but with me you will always have the victory." That day I remembered Jesus' words as I stood before him many years before laying in intensive care, "Sue, you will have children and this will be a sign to the people, a confirmation that you have been to Hell and been to the door of Heaven and spoken with Me. They would say that this experience was a vision, a dream due to the drugs they gave you to save your life, but because of the things I will do in your life they will know without doubt that it has been a true life-changing experience with signs, confirmation, evidence, and proof." I would like to repeat here since it bears repeating, putting the failure behind you is not enough for God! As I stated, there is a moment in our life the finger of God points to the area of defeat and gently leads us back to that place of devastation, and by His love, His grace, His favor, His glory *He annihilates the defeat with overwhelming victory. God knows these areas must be revisited by you and taken over by Him.* God is not a status quo God. Keep in mind; war is about gaining more territory. So what happens after the crushing, the gaining, the victory? The Lord tears down Satan's stronghold, and He builds something beautiful on the very spot Satan claimed. And that was exactly what the Lord had done in my life, right before my eyes. WOW! This day, there was no denying the great display of victory, it could not be reasoned away!

On the way home, my mind flashed back to, the year 1992, the day I brought Elijah home from the hospital. A woman stepped into the hospital elevator, that day, and asked what Elijah's birth date was. My husband answered, "He was born on December 7." She continued, "Oh, Pearl Harbor Day! Do you have any other children?" "Yes," we replied. "What are the dates of their births?" As I answered she smiled a very big smile and said, "How curious, I have never heard of such a thing, you have the World War II Edition. That is unbelievable." Amazingly, the impact of the dates did not hit me until she spoke it and pointed it out. I could see, even then, the Lord was trying to bring to my attention His awesome plan. When I returned home from the Greensboro museum, I read these words in my Bible, "Behold, I and the children whom the Lord hath given me are for signs and wonders... from the Lord of hosts,"(Isaiah 8:18). The NCV Bible says it this way, "I am here (I was in Hell), and with me are the children the Lord has given me (the children I could not have). We are signs and proofs for the people...from the Lord All-powerful." What an awesome God! As I stated before this was a day the Lord would call a marvelous day. What does marvelous mean: tending to arouse wonder or astonishment, superb, excellent, improbable or incredible. Psalm 118:23 says, "This is the Lord's doing; it is marvelous in our eyes." This was truly a day the Lord filled my eyes with wonder.

Before I moved to North Carolina I took the children to a carousel in the town of Fall River. It was a beautiful place and, recently, they had restored an antique carousel, housing it in a beautiful Victorian pavilion. You could hear the sea gulls and feel the sea breeze from the open windows that overlooked the cove. There was a museum we would visit on the boardwalk there. One day, as I stood in the gift shop, I noticed a picture that portrayed the famous Battleship Cove. It evoked childhood memories of collecting money to save the World War II Battleship that sat in the cove. Our class had visited the battleship as a reward for our donations. Now here I was years later at Battleship Cove, in the gift shop of the Fall River Carousel, after the biggest battle of my life, standing with my children, looking at a picture of the carousel (a picture of restoration) and the festivities surrounding it, but in the background sat the Battleship, the picture was called 'Good Times'.

Good Times Print By Artist Karl Doerflinger East Providence, RI

Contact information: Paint4me2@aol.com

It was a poignant moment, a sort of picture of life, a rendering of the fact that before the celebration, there is a battle. I believe the Lord was tapping me on the shoulder, even then, trying to show me that I was living the picture. I had won the war in my life and now I was living in the good times, years later. Another image, in the picture, caught my eye it was a bridge high above spanning across the carousel and the battleship. To me, the bridge represented Jesus, the Way, and the one that bridges the gap from battle to victory. Over and over, I could **see** the Lord's awesome Victory in my life, especially that day, at the Greensboro Museum of History, *it was written* all over the walls of the museum.

Chapter 18

THE GATES OF HELL SHALL NOT PREVAIL

Matthew 16:17,18 tells us the gates of Hell shall not prevail against God's revealed knowledge, or God's spoken word. "For flesh and blood hath not revealed it unto thee, but my Father which is in Heaven. And I say also unto thee, That thou art Peter, and upon this rock I will build my church; and the gates of Hell shall not prevail against it." It is the rock of revelation (God's revealed knowledge) that the gates of Hell shall not prevail against. Revelation causes us to stand, and so we, as Peter, are a rock. God's spoken word makes us immovable, we become a rock ourselves, a kind of smaller rock, a chip off the old rock. For it was by revelation I lived out God's plan for my life. In Daniel 2:28, we are told, "There is a God in Heaven that revealeth secrets, and maketh known." That's what happened to Peter, he received knowledge revealed to him by the Lord, just as I did concerning my life. Revelation was the rock upon which we stood in order to have children, it was the rock upon which we stood in order to complete our house, it was what made us immovable.

My assignment has been to write this book, but not without great difficulty. This year, I have fought a good fight, finished the race, despite attacks, by the enemy, strategically implemented in order to stop this book. 1. I lost the job I loved; 2. The back of my new van was hit while shopping at Wal-Mart; 3. My husband and I needed batteries for our vehicles on the same day; 4.My son was hit in the face with a baseball requiring surgery (but after surgery and before he was transferred to another hospital to have his jaw wired, he was miraculously healed and sent home); 5.A few thousand for hospital bills; 6. Needed a new air conditioning system, $2000; 7. $700 for a check engine light instead of $20 for the sticker; 8. $200 for the dryer (stopped working); 9. George is working a 2nd job again; 10.The computer crashed and wiped out the hard drive; *my completed book could not be retrieved.*

Satan is the master of distractions. Satan's tactics were very familiar, the last time we were in the middle of the house project he tried to sink the boat and put us in a position of losing everything. Jesus speaks in Mark 4:14-20 of Satan's tactics: 1. The enemy presents impossibilities and doubt; 2. He mocks, persecutes and afflicts; 3. He uses financial pressures and concerns. Satan knows the word works and will prevail, so he works at making us weary and trying to make us faint and give up. I remember George saying, we have no money, this house is not complete, it's just a big barn. Matthew 14:25 speaks of the fourth watch, the fourth watch is the darkest hour of the night, and, as with the disciples, can be the most frightening. For it is the time our natural eyes see that we have launched out into the deep (acting on God's spoken word), and we are in the midst of the sea, and *"our promise"*, like a ship, is rocked and tossed, and circumstances, like the wind, are contrary, even strong against us. The fourth watch for many is the moment the hope is deferred, and we now realize we are still in the middle of the sea, our journey is only half done, we are still not yet on the other side. This can be a "staggering" realization. Acts 27:20 says, "And when neither sun nor stars in many days appeared (a dark time) and no small tempest (a stormy time) lay on us, all hope that we should be saved was then taken away." But Acts 27:25 continues, "Wherefore sirs, be of good cheer: for I *believe* **God, that it shall be even as it was told me.**" This is when we must remember Abraham, the Bible says, "He staggered not at the promise of God," Romans 4:20. So it is important to realize that just because we step out on God's spoken word does NOT mean that we will not encounter trouble. We may find ourselves, as Peter, beginning to sink, troubled, afraid, overwhelmed by that which surrounds us, thinking we have stepped out on nothing.

Still, let us not forget, the moment Peter began to sink was also the moment the Lord stretched forth His hand.

The place of difficulty is the place many times the Lord has commanded us to be. Look at Matthew 14:22, "Jesus constrained" his disciples to get into the ship, and to go before him to the other side, knowing they would encounter a storm. Why are we ordered to a place of difficulty? That we, like the disciples, might know when we launch out into the deep, sent out at His word, no matter what befalls us, **His Word is the proven and tried vessel that will carry us to our expected end.** Yes, He asks us not only to launch out, but also launch out into the deep, a place that is way over our heads. So when great darkness falls upon us, and all hope has been taken away, we can be of good cheer for the darkest hour is the place where the Lord meets us and gives us peace in the midst of the storm. Matthew 14:25 says, "In the fourth watch of the night Jesus went unto them."

If we hold on to God's Word we do get to the other side. Revelation is the rock upon which we stand; it is the sure word, the sure vessel. Still, we are warned repeatedly in scripture to be strong and courageous. We are told not to be afraid and not to allow our courage to be stripped away. Why? Because there will be opportunities to be afraid, and to be dismayed and we need to be armed with the Word and prepared for battle.

We must be filled with the Word of God. Exodus 12:10,11, says, "And ye shall **let nothing of it remain**...And thus shall ye eat it; (the Lamb, the Word of God) with 1. **your loins girded** 2. **your shoes on your feet** and 3. **your staff in your hand (power)**; and ye shall eat it in haste: it is the Lord's Passover (it is by His Word we Passover). Note in this scripture, concerning Passover, it has a striking resemblance to God's Armour in Ephesians, chapter 6:14-17, "Stand therefore, 1. **having your loins girt about with truth (the word of God)**, and having on the breastplate of righteousness; And 2. **your feet shod with the preparation of the gospel** of peace; Above all, taking the shield of faith, wherewith ye shall be able to quench all the fiery darts of the wicked. And take unto you the helmet of salvation, and 3. **the sword of**

the Spirit, which is the word of God (power)."

- Loins girded: Strengthened in the inner man, courage gathered, ready to run with the truth (the Word).

- Feet shod: Standing on the truth, in peace and without fear, prepared to carry out the revelation (the Word).

- Your staff (or sword) in your hand: Stretching out your hand, in power, against the enemy, using the Word of God to cut him off.

- Jesus was very clear when I was in His presence emphasizing the importance of the Word, He said in John 6:63, "The words I speak unto you, they are **spirit, and they are life**." His words have life in them, power in them, the ability in them to come to pass. When Jesus (during the coma) said, "Behold," and a mirror appeared before me, and I looked into it and saw my future, I did not know the mirror represented the Bible. Since then I have realized that, like a mirror, when we look into the Bible, we see things about ourselves, and through the Spirit we see things concerning our life, we receive instruction and direction and we even see our future. Did you know that is why Satan uses a **crystal** ball to tell the future? It is his imitation of the Holy Sprit. The book of Revelation 22:1 speaks of the Holy Spirit saying, "And he shewed me a pure river of water of life, **clear as crystal**, proceeding out of the throne of God and of the Lamb," and John 16:13 tells us the **Spirit will show you things to come**. Yet, many people have been so afraid of the Holy Spirit (or Holy Ghost) that they have left themselves powerless. They have become what I call Brylcreem Christians. Brylcreem was a sort of hair gel or oil in the 1950's and the slogan was "A little dab will do ya." I am here to tell you that a dab will not do ya. We need to cry out like David and ask the Lord to pour out that overflowing cup of oil all over our heads. 1 John 2:27 says, "But the *anointing (oil)* which ye have received of him abideth in you, and *ye need not that any man teach you*: but as the same anointing teacheth you of all things, and is truth, and is no lie, and even as it hath taught you, ye shall abide in him," for it is by the outpouring of His Spirit we **see** things!

In this book, "You Shall See With Your Eyes," I share seeing illuminated scriptures, words or letters in my mind, mental pictures that serve to solve problems, lead, guide or cause success. Satan covets this gift he does not have it, he cannot reveal truth because he is a liar (refer John 8:44). Satan hates revelation because the gates of Hell cannot prevail against it. When I was in Satan's presence, he mocked the things of God. He mocks revelation, prophecy, and the Spirit, because that is how we **see!** Satan wants to keep us blindfolded. Luke 22:63-65 says, "And the men that held Jesus **mocked him**, and smote him. And when they had **blindfolded him**, they struck him on the face, and asked him saying, **Prophesy** (reveal to us), **who is it that smote thee**? And many other things blasphemously spake they against him." That is why when Jesus was in Satan's power (as Jesus said in Luke 22:53 "But this is your hour, and the power of darkness.") Satan, through the Roman soldiers mocked and blasphemed revelation and prophecy. Jesus wore Satan's blindfold for us, so that now, we are able to see. Revelation is powerful, precious, and valuable. Satan hates it, because it is the thing Hell can't beat. Genesis 41:25, "God hath shewed...what He is about to do."

Matthew 27:41 tells us, they mocked Jesus on the cross. Mark 15:29 says, "And they that passed by railed on him, wagging their heads." Whenever you are doing something as a result of God's spoken word, Satan will send the mockers. Satan will get people to mock you at your most vulnerable times, while you're doing the work of God. My son Elijah's birth was mocked, "When's Abraham, Isaac, Jacob, or whatever his name coming?" The house (the museum of faith) was mocked, "How's the house?" Day after day this question was mockingly asked, during the toughest time of our life. The Bible says, we fight not against flesh and blood, but against spiritual wickedness. This book tells the story of His Glory. Now everyone can see Elijah has come! Now everyone knows how the house is. The Bible tells us, Galatians 6:7,9 that **God is not**

mocked, especially by Satan, for in due season *we will reap* **a great reward**, if we faint not!

I would like to take the time to say, thanks to my brother, Jeff. Thanks for everything! It is at this time I express to you my deepest gratitude and thanks for being a brother that stuck closer than any brother would, you made me laugh at that crazy question that was used over and over as a greeting, "How's the house?" You helped us with so much, and at that time, took time off as an Operations Manager to roll up your sleeves and tackle construction and so much more. You moved out and gave me your apartment, talk about going the extra mile. What an awesome brother you are! And to my wonderful husband, George, the modern day Noah, I love you, what a man! I must say, "Very impressive."

Job 33:14-16 says, "For God speaketh once, yea twice, yet man perceiveth it not. In a dream, in a vision of the night, when deep sleep falleth upon men, in slumberings upon the bed; Then he openeth the ears of men, and sealeth their instructions." When God speaks, stuff happens! Ecclesiastes 8:4, "Where the word of a king is, there is power." The Holy Spirit is the power that turns on the vision, like television, your eyes will see, your ears will hear, the things God has prepared for you will enter your heart. Instead of seeing useless things, you see things that bring success, things that guide you in your life. The Bible tells us to harness the mind by casting down imaginations. What are imaginations? They are false images, images of failure, empty mental pictures, empty visions, empty thinking, thinking that is void of life and truth. 2 Corinthians 10:4 says, "Casting down imaginations, and every high thing that exalteth itself against **the knowledge (word) of God,** and bringing into captivity every thought to the obedience of Christ." Daniel 2:45, "The great God hath made known...what shall come to pass, hereafter: and the dream is certain, and the interpretation thereof sure." God's information is certain and sure! The question we must ask, is the one Jesus asked, "Was it from Heaven, or of men? Answer me?" We must get our information from God. Genesis

41:16, "It is not in me; God shall give...an answer of peace."

We are told throughout Matthew, chapter 2, of warnings given, words given, examples of knowledge from God. Here is a list of examples from my life:

- God's revealed Word: Isaiah 55 Result: Filled with the Holy Spirit and power

- God's revealed Word: John 11:4 Result: Healed of a disease

- God's revealed Word: Isaiah 54 Result: Children

- God's revealed Word: 2 Samuel 2:1 Result: Took the roof off

- God's revealed Word Isaiah 54:2 Result: Enlarged our house (Ranch to Garrison).

- God's revealed Word Genesis 24:29 Result: A son Elijah

- God's revealed Word 2 Corinthians 2:14 Result: Great display of victory

- God's revealed Word John 11:40 Results: This book

God's supernatural Word always prevails against the enemy. The Lord, through the Word, not only prevailed, but annihilated Satan's plan for my life, blew up all the enemy had built and destroyed his lies, traps, and snares. Not only did the Lord, by His Word, defeat the enemy in my life, but He took my life and turned it into a showcase of **Victory**! 1 Corinthians 12:7,8 says, "But the *manifestation of the Spirit* is given to every man to profit withal. For to one is given by the Spirit *the word of wisdom*; to another *the word of knowledge*, by the same Spirit." 1 Corinthians 14:3 tells us about building words, words that build us up, warning words, words to protect us, and words of comfort. What is so important about these words? They are supernatural words that are weapons for our warfare. A Supernatural Word, a revealed word from the Lord is your Supernatural-**WORD**! And when you use your **Sword** you will *see* the gates of Hell shall not prevail.

Chapter 19

AND NOT REASON

Years ago, the Lord gave me a prophecy pertaining to my personal life, "They shall *see* with their eyes the glory of the Living God and they shall not reason." Immediately thereafter confirming it with the scripture, John 11:40, "Said I not unto thee if thou wouldest believe thou shouldest *see* the Glory of God?" This book, these events, are a display of God's Glory, so that many might *see* through 1.the written word; 2.His given word (or spoken word to me); and 3.pictures (fulfillment of that given word)); that God is a truthful God, a very good God, a great God. Seeing is very important to God, He wants us to see clearly. 1 Corinthians 2:9,10 clearly tells us that, "Eye hath not seen, nor ear heard, neither have entered into the heart of man, the things which God hath prepared for them that love him. But *God hath revealed them unto us by his Spirit*. (Or caused us to *see* by his Spirit.)" As I explained in another book, **The Golden Thread,** God sent His Holy Spirit so we might *see* clearly. The Holy Spirit gives us the power to *see.* Many people do not understand that when we read the Bible through man's eyes, we get distortion (opinions), whereas the Holy Spirit defines. The Holy Spirit is the glass (or lens) the spiritual man looks through in order to see clearly (the truth). Somehow, people have tried to portray the Holy Spirit (or Holy Ghost) as spooky. Let me ask you a question; is a pair of glasses spooky, or do you enjoy seeing? Satan's objective is to cause us **not to** *see.* 2 Corinthians 4:4 says, "The god of this world (referring to Satan) hath **blinded** the minds of them which believe not." *Satan* *does not want us to see*, so if he cannot blind the mind, he will settle for a veil, or dark glasses that we might have a distorted view and image of God and the truth. Satan likes to cover things in darkness so that we have trouble seeing. Previously, I shared some of my experiences in Hell. Since that time, I have had a better understanding of Satan's tactics in this world. One of the things I experienced was Satan taking off his black velvet cape and covering me with darkness **when the Lord spoke to me**. Satan does not want us to see the truth. Why? Truth sets us free, and his goal is that we remain in darkness with no light.

One day, when I was having a rough day, I noticed a sign I went by on a regular basis had lost a letter. It was a rental sign that was in front of a church called Victory. So, whenever I passed by that sign I would rejoice and say thank you for the Victory! But this day, sadness came over me as I looked at the word on the sign with the missing letter. I felt that I had lost my victory along with the missing letter. Suddenly, the Holy Spirit rose up in me and said, "Look! Look at the sign!" I looked at that sign; the

"**Y**" was the missing letter. The Holy Spirit continued, "I am calling you a Victor!" What a revelation. Our flesh naturally feels sad in a sad situation, and the enemy manipulates our circumstances to confirm our feelings, he comes to cover us with darkness, but God reveals the truth by His Spirit. God invades our darkness with light and good news canceling out the bad news. The scriptures tell us where God's Spirit is, there is liberty.

Truth opposes Satan's kingdom of darkness, because truth sheds light, it *uncovers*. Isaiah 60 tells us, "that darkness shall *cover* the earth and gross darkness the people," we are urged to arise and shine, taking our place, especially in dark times. Why? When darkness covers the Earth, people have trouble seeing God. Satan's strategy during these times is to affect our circumstances hoping that we pay more attention to the things surrounding us than we do to God. The enemy wants us caught up with the world's disparity so that our light is dimmed, but we are called to be very bright lights dispelling darkness in dark times, always remembering that light prevails. When light enters the room, darkness flees, it is pushed back, or obliterated; moreover, it is important to note that light is seen better in darkness.

I have said many times in my preaching that the position of profound difficulty is the platform for the display (show) of His Almighty power and grace, and as you can *see,* through my life, that statement is very true! This book is a display of His Glory, of His Victory in my life, a true demonstration of the Spirit and a demonstration of power. I too, like Paul, can say, "And my speech and my preaching was not with enticing words of man's wisdom, but in demonstration of the Spirit and of power: That your faith should not stand in the wisdom of men but in the power of God," 1 Corinthians 2:4,5. In this book you see a lot of supernatural evidence. What some might call the effects of the blowing of the Spirit in my life, the same thing the Lord was talking about with Nicodemus in John 3:8. You cannot see the Spirit, which he likened to the wind; but you do **see** the effects like the moving of the leaves.

I believe this book is a testimony to the fact that the "just shall live by faith (or confidence in God.)" I have been around many religious men, as Jesus was around the Pharisees, but the difference was they were religious and He was powerful. It was evident Jesus had been with God. John 9:33, "If this man were not of God, he could do nothing." People can tell when you have been with God. Still, more important than all this is, through this book, the mission Jesus gave me is fulfilled. My mission was to return, and tell about my experience in Hell, and my experience with Him and Heaven, and He would confirm it. Jesus fulfilled all His promises, all the evidence, the proof, the signs, including healing me so I could have children, literally raising me from the dead, when I was on life-support systems. I have to be truthful with you, when Jesus said, "Behold" and I looked into the mirror and saw my future, I did not believe it was possible, even though He was showing it to me. How could it happen? It all seemed impossible. My mind could not wrap itself around all Jesus was telling me, all He was showing me. As you read 1 Corinthians, chapter 2, it explains it all. The natural man *cannot receive or see* with his spiritual eyes because he is blind to all the great things God wants to do for him. My feelings of blindness were true at that time; I was blind to the things of God. I was as blind Bartimeus, even a spiritual beggar, begging God for crumbs when He wanted to give me the whole loaf. Even my garment was a beggar's garment, when I stood before him, a beggar's garment of filthy rags. In Isaiah 64:6, we are told that all our good works in the flesh are as filthy rags. At that time I had not been born of God (Born Again) or of the Spirit. What makes a man a father of a child is that the man has given that child life. I was not yet a child of God, I lived in the kingdom of darkness, which every person does, until, they give their life to the Lord and are translated to the kingdom of light. I truly believed that it was God preventing me from having children because I could not see, I did not understand. Jesus tells us, "Except a man be born again, he **cannot see,**" John 3:3. I was blind.

Do you know our understanding has eyes? Isn't that awesome? God's will is that we see, that the eyes of our understanding are enlightened, or opened, so we can see and understand concerning all the great things He has prepared for us. Ephesians 1:17-19 says, "That the God of our Lord Jesus Christ, the Father of glory, may give unto you the spirit of wisdom and revelation in the knowledge of him: The **eyes of your understanding** being enlightened; that *ye may know* what is the hope of his calling, and what the riches of the glory of his inheritance in the saints, And what is the exceeding greatness of his power to usward who believe according to the working of his mighty power."

It was an amazing thing to realize that the Lord wanted me to have children. Matthew 16:17 says, "For flesh and blood hath not revealed it unto thee, but my Father which is in Heaven." When I was in Hell, Satan wanted me to fall down and worship him, Satan was proudly trying to impress me with his ability to give life and I did not understand or see what he was doing. You see, he had targeted an area of my life to bring death, failure, and defeat; I could not have children. That was his plan, to steal my life, destroy my life and finally kill me. He even tried to get me to bow before him and worship him, saying he would reveal hidden secrets to me. Those are 2 things the Lord has done in my life: given life to me (given me children) and revealed many things that were hidden from me. Satan did not have the ability to give me the things he was promising. Why? He did not have that power.

As Satan stood in his parlor of death, dressed in midnight black, staring at me with his prideful, mocking eyes, I saw him as extremely religious. He brought me to the Book of the Law and opened it. Yes, Satan has a Book in Hell, just as Jesus has the Book of Life in Heaven. It is the Book of the Law, (Revelation 12:9,10 tells us The Devil, Satan, is the accuser, he accuses day and night); Satan uses it for judgment and death! Satan knows the written word very well, like an unscrupulous lawyer, his purpose is to deceive, to twist, and distort the word. Satan is, as the scriptures state, a liar. Remember, he presented himself to me as a magician that is a trickster, an illusionist, a deceiver.

All Satan showed me was very unappealing. His dwelling place was full of death, fear, and darkness, a combination funeral parlor and very ornate, overdone, religious shrine with golden goblets and a golden altar with the horns and heads of rams. Then, I was led by his little gargoyle minions relentlessly and irritatingly chattering, as they led me to Satan's throne room. The room was the color of pewter, and the scent of the room was dank and musty. The throne was the gray of a graveyard headstone; the throne room had the atmosphere of a gloomy, cloudy day. When I would not bow, or drink of the goblet, or obey any of Satan's commands I found myself suddenly at the Gates of Hell. The gates were very large. They were gray made seemingly with pipes mounted on steel arrows. The pipes seemed to emit sounds of misery, a sort of death march song. As I surveyed the landscape, it appeared to resemble an old deserted steel mill, or a muddy dump; the sky above was smoky and polluted. People were in the dump, wallowing in mud, reaching out, calling accompanied by sighs and cries of misery and pain.

All this was totally opposite to Heaven, the Heaven I saw behind Jesus was beautiful, unlike Hell, with no trace of religiosity, only beautiful meadows, and beautiful flowers, beautiful blue skies, chirping birds, soft, serene, simple, quiet, safe, and beautiful. What was the sound of Heaven you might ask? The sound of Heaven was sweet laughter, and cheerful gentle voices, like the sound of happy people at the beach.

As I previously stated, Satan tried to present himself to me as an angel of light, proudly stating, "I can give life," as he stood by the caskets with his rod tapping the caskets. He was very impressed with himself and his so-called abilities, feigning the ability to give life, as if raising the dead. He could give no life to the dead in the caskets, his rod is dead, only God and man have the power to give and create life. That is why the union of a man and woman is so important in the sight of God. They have the power to create an eternal being, a living soul that will live forever in Heaven or Hell. It is sad that we who are made in the image of God take this so lightly when even Satan covets the power himself and realizes its importance. Nevertheless, Satan has a magician's power, a kind of special effects certainly not the kind of awesome power the Holy Spirit gives. That is why 1 John 4:4 says, "Greater is He

that is in you than he that is in the world."
Ours is a dynamite power, an outwardly
visible power, as you saw in this book, a
power that enables us to accomplish a
supernatural task. It is God, the super, joined
to us, the natural, accomplishing the
impossible. God anoints us and we become
divinely empowered. Ephesians 3:20 says,
"Now unto Him that is able to do exceeding
abundantly above all that we ask or think,
according to the power that worketh in us."

Here are some important points concerning
Heaven and Hell, Jesus and Satan:

Jesus

- Speaks to save us He said, "Open the door."

- He is gentle, I heard a soft sweet voice as that of an angel

- He speaks truth, when I opened the door I went to Heaven

- Everything Jesus told me and showed me was confirmed by scriptures when I returned (remember at this time I did not understand the Bible, it was as Chinese to me, I had no idea what the Scriptures said)

- He is the Door and the Light, as I stood before Him He was the Door and He was Light

Satan

- Tries to trick and deceive, he appeared as a magician

- He is the god of thick darkness, he took off his cape and enveloped me in heavy darkness

- He is an illusionist and the god of confusion, he caused three doors to appear when there was only one

- He is a liar and the master of fear, a terrorist; he said if you choose the wrong door you shall surely die!

I think it is important to note that we have the power! Satan has no power unless we give it to him by yielding to him. Even in Hell, I had a choice, to bow, to drink blood, to fear, to yield to his commands. Concerning Jesus, I had to Hear His voice, See what He was saying, Overcome fear, and obey His Word.

Satan's objective is to thwart the plan of God. It is evident that Hell tried vigorously to stop God's plan and fought with great fervor concerning the plan for my life. Satan was so close to succeeding in foiling the plan, considering I was in his grasp when I was in Hell. I am so thankful that the Lord has let me know, through His signs and wonders in my life, that He knew and was well aware that I was not just in a battle, but an all-out war. 1 Thessalonians 2:18 says, "Satan hindered us." Satan did not prevent us, but he sure caused difficulty. Satan never wanted people to see the great and mighty things God had accomplished in my life. As I shared earlier, in 1982, the Lord gave me the prophecy, "They shall 'see' with their eyes the glory of the living God and **they shall not reason**." Then confirming the prophecy with, John 11:40, "Said I not unto thee, if thou wouldest believe, thou shouldest 'see' the glory of God?" Yet, this scripture is dealing with raising the dead, a wonder, a miracle, specifically a man who had been dead four days and would stink. So what is the point you may ask? What does the Bible say after Jesus raised Lazarus? *"And many* *which had 'seen' the things which Jesus did, believed."* That is the point! Many times when people see wondrous things, **they believe**, this book is full of wondrous things.

I challenge you today to diligently seek God, calling out to Him, believing He will answer and show you great and mighty things. Yes, 1 Corinthians 2:9,10 says, "But as it is written, Eye hath not seen nor ear heard, neither have entered into the heart of man, the things which God hath prepared for them that love him. *But God hath revealed them (the great and mighty things) unto us by His Spirit.*" Joel 2:28, says, "I will pour out My Spirit upon all flesh; and your sons and your daughters shall *prophesy* **(see),** your old men shall *dream **dreams*** **(see),** your young men shall *see **visions*** **(see)**. Even upon the men servants and upon the maidservants in those days will I pour out My Spirit? And I will *show (cause to see)* wonders."

I believe, in the midst of these difficult times, this book has come forth with light so that people might feel empowered, by God, to be warriors of light knowing that God still does great and mighty things through and for His people. It is amazing how fiercely Satan fought to get me, and he almost succeeded, how very close he was. The fact that Satan fought so relentlessly and with such great fervor testifies to the fact he never wanted this story to be told. Years ago, had Satan had his way in my life, I would have died hopeless, childless, and defeated, all that would have seemed true, yet although those were the facts, it was not the truth. Exodus 7:11,12 says, "Then Pharaoh also called the wise men and the sorcerers: now the magicians of Egypt, they also did in like manner with their enchantments. For they cast down every man his rod, and they became serpents: but Aaron's rod swallowed up their rods." Just as Aaron's rod swallowed up the magician's rods, so too in my life, death and defeat were swallowed up in victory. 1 Corinthians 15:57 says, "Thanks be to God, which giveth us the victory through our Lord Jesus Christ." Verse 54 says, "Death is swallowed up in victory." Verse 55 asks, "O death where is thy sting? O grave, where is thy victory?" God's plan was that I would have children, a great testimony, and a great victorious life, but, if I had died that day, the truth would never have been displayed. Acts 26:18 says, "Now I send thee, To **open their eyes**, and to turn them from **darkness to light**, and **from the power of Satan unto God**."

Matthew 13:16 says, "*Blessed are your eyes, for they see*." It is my prayer that this book has blessed you and that you do *see* God in all that was done and that you will not be as Luke 16:19 says, "Neither will they be persuaded though one rose from the dead." As I said from the beginning, I was sent back to testify to you. The world has opinions God has truth. Many, including pastors, have gone so far as to say, Hell is not for real and it does not exist. Hell is mentioned 54 times in the Bible, and described and referred to in other ways, such as a place of weeping and gnashing of teeth, outer darkness, etc. These pastors, for popularity's sake, preach, there is no Hell, when the Bible says there is a Hell, and they preach that **most** shall go to Heaven, when the Bible says, **few**. Mark 9:43-48 goes into great lengths to warn about the horror and seriousness of Hell. Galatians 1:7-12 says, "**Even if an Angel from Heaven preaches to you another gospel, let him be**

accursed!!!" The Bible is the measuring stick of truth. Revelation 22:18,19 warns, If any man shall add; if any man shall take away, there are severe consequences. John 1:14, "The Word (referring to Jesus) was made Flesh and dwelt among us." Jesus is the A and the Z. You cannot add to him, you cannot subtract from him. Revelation 19:13 says, "His name is THE WORD OF GOD." Jesus warns in Matthew 24:4,24, "Take heed that no man deceive you.... IF it were possible, they shall deceive the very elect." God uses a qualifier, IF! If we know the scriptures, the Word of God, we shall not be deceived! God conducts His business as a courtroom: witnesses, testimony, eyewitness reports, confirmation, evidence, proofs, document-ation, and yes, even; judges. 1 Corinthians 14:29, "Let the prophets speak two or three, and let the other judge." And 1 Corinthians 6:3, "Know ye not that we shall judge angels? How much more things that pertain to this life?" We judge not according to our opinion, but according to the Word. Like earthly judges, it must be according to **the book of the law**(The Bible). 2 Timothy 2:15

says, "Study to shew thyself approved." The world has opinions; God has truth!

I present in this book the Evidence, Proofs, and Confirmation according to the book of the Law. Below are listed the things I experienced that were confirmed by scripture.

- Thick Darkness / Matthew 8:12 Outer Darkness

- Fear/ God hath **not** given us a spirit of fear. 2 Timothy 1:7 Fear has torment 1 John 4:18

- Falling/ Bottomless pit Revelation 20:1,3

- Black Curtain/ Curtains in the tabernacle Numbers 4:25

- Horns of the altar/ Leviticus 4:18

- Death, caskets, / Revelation 1:18 Jesus said, the keys of Death of Hell.

- Covered in darkness/ Isaiah 60:2 Gross darkness

- Gates of Hell /Matthew 16:18

- Magician/ Exodus 7:10-12 Illusions, trickery and deceit/ Revelation 12:9 says, "Satan which deceiveth the whole world."

- Magician's rod/ Exodus 7:12 /Moses' rod swallowed up the magician's rod. The rod is sign of power, life and God given approval/ Living rod trumped the dead rods, Aaron's rod blossomed/ Numbers 17:5-10

- Mocking/ Galatians 6:7 "Be not deceived; God is not mocked."

- Golden altar /2 Chronicles 4:19

- Blood/ Acts 15:20, "Abstain from ...blood."

- Bow and worship, seeks worship/Luke 4:7, "If thou therefore wilt worship me, all shall be thine."

- You will surely die! / John 8:44, "He was a murderer from the beginning, and abode not in the truth, because there is no truth in him. When he speaketh a lie, he speaketh of his own: for he is a liar, and the father of it."

- Demons/ James 2:19, "Thou believest that there is one God; thou doest well: the devils also believe, and tremble." Jude 6 is clear, "And the angels which kept not their first estate, but left their own habitation, he hath reserved in everlasting chains under darkness unto the judgment of the great day." Revelation 12:9, "Satan...was cast out into the earth, and his angels were cast out with him."

- Lawyer/ uses the Law against us Revelation 12:9,10 says, Satan...accuses us before God day and night.

- Doors /Satan has doors, many ways. He that entereth not by **The** Door into the sheepfold, but climeth up some other way, the same is a thief and a robber." Jesus is the only Way!

- Blind /Acts 26:18, "To open their eyes, and to turn them from darkness to light, and from the power of Satan unto God."

- Like a ball through space/ Ephesians 4:9,10 I descended and ascended

- Light pierced the darkness/ John 1:9 tells us Jesus was the "true Light."

- The Door /Jesus himself says, "I am the Door." John 10:7

- Love, fear obliterated/ There is no fear in Love. 1 John 4:18

- The Word/ John 1:14 says, "And the Word was made flesh."

- Truth/ Jesus says, "I am the Way, the Truth, and the life: no man cometh unto the Father, but by me."

- Natural man/ 2 Corinthians 2:14, "But the natural man receiveth not the things of the Spirit of God; for they are foolishness unto him."

- The rays of light from Jesus/ Galatians 5:22, "The fruit of the Spirit is love, joy, peace, longsuffering, gentleness, goodness, faith, meekness, temperance."

- Filthy rags/ Isaiah 64:6 says, "But we are all as an unclean thing, and all our righteousnesses are as filthy rags." Filthy garments/ Zechariah 3:3,4

- Born Again/ John 3:3,6, "Verily, verily, I say unto thee, Except a man be born again, he **cannot see** the kingdom of God.... That which is born of the flesh is flesh; and that which is born of the Spirit is spirit."

- Seeing and Hearing and Showing me things/ John 16:12,13, "I have yet many things to say unto you, but ye cannot bear them now. Howbeit when he, the Spirit of truth is come, he will guide you into all truth....and shew you things to come."

- Mirror (Behold)/ The Bible 2 Corinthians 3:18, "But we all with open face beholding as in a glass (or Mirror) the glory of the Lord, are changed into the same image."

Evidence and Proof Upon Return

1. Understanding the Bible

2. The sign of blood on my Bible

3. Filled with the Holy Spirit with the evidence of tongues

4. A word of knowledge

5. Healed from Reynaud's Disease

6. Supernatural answers to unanswered questions

7. Causing demons to speak and react/ seeing into the spiritual realm

8. Experiencing supernatural protection (Angels)

9. Healed (no longer barren) 3 children

10. Receiving wisdom and instruction from the Lord

11. Isaiah 54 Enlarge thy tent, Ranch to a Garrison

12. Receiving signs for direction

13. Elijah, my son, Genesis 24:29

14. Prophecy fulfilled John 11:40

15. Extreme care from the Lord in moving, "Regard not your stuff." Genesis 45:20

16. Extreme and overwhelming victory

17. Display of victory at the **Greensboro Museum of History:** newspapers, broadsheets, headlines, birth dates in bold type on the walls! (World War II Anniversary)

21.**Children's Birth Dates:** Birth Certificates are **official documents** serving as evidence or testimony 12/7, 8/14, 12/7 Pearl Harbor Day, Victory Day, Pearl Harbor Day (World War II Edition)

Chapter 20

CAUTION TAPE

At this point, I caution you not to risk living forever in Hell, based on your opinion or anyone else's. Research it through Scripture for yourself. I believe it is God's intention, through this book and its evidence, to put out the yellow caution tape, warning all of the very real danger and reality of Hell.

In the Bible, a rich man desired that someone from the dead would warn his family concerning Hell. Luke 16:28-31, "For I have five brethren; that he may **testify** unto them, lest they also come into this place of **torment (Hell)**. Abraham saith unto him, they have Moses and the prophets; let them hear them. And he said, Nay, father Abraham: but **if one went unto them from the dead**, they will repent. And he said unto him, If they hear not Moses and the prophets, neither will they be persuaded, **though one rose from the dead.**"

The Mission: To let you know the Bible is true and exact! Hell is a real place and Heaven is a real place! That's my mission! My testimony is true and I am an eyewitness.

All pictures are actual with the exception of pictures in Chapter 1 and Chapter 2. I could not bring my camera with me into the spiritual realm.

If this book has been a blessing to you, please let me know.

Sue Laprise
PO Box 3224
Asheboro, NC. 27204

suelaprise@embarqmail.com

PRAYER FOR SALVATION AND BAPTISM IN THE HOLY SPIRIT

Heavenly Father, I come to You in the name of Jesus. Your Word says, " For whosoever shall call upon the Name of the Lord shall be saved," Romans 10:13 I am calling upon You, and turning away from my sins, forgive me. I ask you, Jesus to come into my heart and be Lord of my life according to Romans 10:9-10: "That if thou shalt confess with thy mouth the Lord Jesus, and shalt believe in thine heart that God raised him from the dead, thou shalt be saved. For with the heart man believeth unto righteousness; and with the mouth confession is made unto salvation." So I confess that Jesus is Lord, and I believe in my heart that God raised him from the dead. I ask you to cleanse my heart of all unrighteousness, and give me a clean, fresh start. Help me to strive for a close relationship with you, by reading my Bible every day, and talking to you in prayer. Thank you, Lord! Now, I am born again! I am a child of God! I am saved! You also said in Your Word, "If ye then, being evil, know how to give good gifts unto your children; how much more shall your heavenly Father give the Holy Spirit to them that ask him?" Luke 11:13 I ask You now to fill me with your Holy Spirit. Holy Spirit come and fill me to overflowing. You said in Psalms 81:10, "Open thy mouth wide, and I will fill it." And Romans 8:15, "Ye have received the Spirit of adoption, whereby we cry, **Abba,** Father." As I thank you Lord, and praise you, I expect to speak with other tongues as you give me the utterance (refer Acts 2:4). In Jesus name I pray. Amen!

About The Author

Sue Laprise, who was born in Boston, Massachusetts, is a speaker, teacher, and writer, sharing and teaching the Word of God since 1981. She has appeared on several television shows sharing her amazing testimony. Her desire is for people to know that their circumstances are not the "measuring stick" concerning whether God is real or not. Gauging God's existence by our circumstances is dangerous and will repeatedly lead us to the wrong answer! Jesus told us to pray that His "will be done in earth as it is in Heaven" (refer Matt. 6:10), so we know from this, His will is not automatically accomplished on Earth. As Sue found out, as an atheist and kept alive only by a respirator, even if you do not believe something is true or exists, concerning forever, it is too dangerous to be wrong. Finding herself in Hell a place she did not believe existed and confronted by a devil she had no idea was real and standing before a Lord she did not believe in. Her cry and warning is, "Don't make a mistake!" Forever is a long time to be in torment. If you do not like talking about Hell, you definitely won't like being there. Hell is far worse than anyone can imagine. Jesus, himself, warned us of its severity by saying, "It is better for thee to enter into life maimed than...to go into Hell, into the fire that never shall be quenched: where their worm dieth not, and the fire is not quenched." (refer Mark 9:43-48). We choose! In Heaven, there is no death, in Heaven, there is no darkness, in Heaven, there is no fear, in Heaven, there is no sickness, in Heaven, there is no lack, in Heaven, there is no hate, in Heaven, there is no torment, in Heaven, there is no sadness, just Love, Joy, Peace and Righteousness. Where do you want to be? This book, "You Shall See With Your Eyes", definitely gives you something to think about! Sue continues to fulfill her mission through speaking, teaching and writing in order to touch and save lives by exposing the truth concerning Heaven and Hell, God and Satan. Sue and her husband, George, are the parents of three grown children and make their home in Asheboro, North Carolina.

Coming Soon, the new book:

THE PRESENT

The Greatest Most Powerful Precious Gift
SUE LAPRISE

Do you feel lost? Don't know where you're going? Get out your heavenly GPS, plug it in and let God set your coordinates. When you follow His directions, His instructions, His signs...you will be exactly where you should be! A place of Peace, Victory, Joy, Love, Prosperity and Blessing! Remember follow Him! He will lead you to certain victory in all areas of life!

A SPECIAL PREVIEW CHAPTER

Chapter 1
THE GIFT

What is the gift? The gift is the Holy Spirit according to Acts 2:38. And who doesn't get excited about receiving a gift, especially a gift from God! God loves us and wants to give us good and perfect gifts, and the Holy Spirit is that good gift, that perfect gift. Moreover, it is a gift of power, Acts 1:8 tells us, "But ye shall receive **power** after that the Holy Ghost is come upon you." We need power in our lives, yet you might ask, what is power? 1. Ability; 2. Strength; 3. Authority; 4. Influence; 5. Energy; 6. Multiplying; 7. The Magnifying of a lens, or other optical lens, power to see; 8. Power as electricity. Now ask yourself, could I use more ability, strength, authority, influence, energy, increase, clarity, and electricity in my life? As we read further we can see the drastic difference between the natural man, and the spiritual man.

✓   Jesus says to the **natural** man, "Ye worship ye know not what." John 4:22 But of the **spiritual** man he says, "We know what we worship...the hour cometh, and now is, when the true worshippers shall worship the Father in spirit and in truth; for the Father seeketh such to worship him. God is a Spirit: and they that worship him must worship him in spirit and in truth." John 4:23, 24

✓   To the **natural** man the Scriptures say, "The things of God knoweth no man." 1 Corinthians 2:11 But to the **spiritual** man the Scriptures say, "God hath revealed them (the things of God) unto us by his Spirit." 1 Corinthians 2:10

✓   Of the **natural** man the Scriptures tell us, "Eye hath not seen, nor ear heard, neither have entered into the heart of man, the things which God hath prepared for them that love him." 1 Corinthians 2:9 But of the **spiritual** man Jesus says, "Blessed are your eyes, for they see: and your ears, for they hear. For verily I say unto you, that many prophets and righteous men have desired to see those things which ye see, and have not seen them; and to hear those things

which ye hear, and have not heard them."
Matthew 13:16, 17

✓ Of the **natural** man the Scriptures say, "The natural man receiveth not the things of the Spirit of God." 1 Corinthians 2:14 But of the **spiritual** man, "Now we have received...the spirit which is of God; that we might know the things that are freely given to us of God." 1 Corinthians 2:12

✓ Jesus asks the **natural** man that is a religious leader, "Art thou a master...and knowest not these things?" And of the **spiritual** man, he says, "We do know." John 3:10, 11

✓ Jesus says of the **natural** man, "Ye know not what ye ask." Matthew 20:22 Concerning the **spiritual** man, Romans 8:26 says, "The Spirit itself maketh intercession…according to the will of God."

✓ Of the **natural** man concerning revelation Jesus says, "Flesh and blood hath not revealed...The flesh profiteth nothing." Matthew 16:17 and John 6:63. Of the **spiritual** man the Scriptures say, "God hath revealed...unto us by his Spirit." 1 Corinthians 2:10

✓ Of the **natural** man concerning peace Jesus says, "If thou hadst known, even thou, at least in this thy day, the things which belong unto thy

peace! But now they are hid from thine eyes."
Luke 19:42   But to the **spiritual** man he says,
"Peace I leave with you, my peace I give unto
you: not as the world giveth, give I unto you.
Let not your heart be troubled, neither let it be
afraid...The Comforter, which is the Holy Ghost,
whom the Father will send in my name, he shall
teach you all things, and bring all things to your
remembrance, whatsoever I have said unto you."
John 14:26,27

✓   Of the **natural** man Jesus says, "To them it is
not given...to know the mysteries of the kingdom
of heaven."   But, of the **spiritual** man, Jesus
says, "It is given unto you to know the mysteries
of the kingdom of heaven." Matthew 13:11

✓   Of the **natural** man Ecclesiastes 8:7 says,
"He knoweth not." Of the **spiritual** man 1 John
2:20 says,"Ye have an unction from the Holy
One, and ye know all things.

✓   Of the **natural** man John 15:15 says, "For the
servant knoweth not what his lord doeth."   Of
the **spiritual** man verse 15 continues, "but I have
called you friends; for all things that I have heard
of my Father I have made known unto you."

179

✓ We see through the Scriptures it is by God's Spirit that all men are converted (Matthew 13:15), from natural to supernatural. The **natural man** is as a house without power (or electricity). The **spiritual man** has power! What could this power in the spiritual man's life be compared to in the natural man's life?

1. The spiritual man is as a natural man using a television. John 16:13,14, "The Spirit of truth...will shew you things to come...he...shall shew it unto you." The Spirit enables us to see and hear spiritually. The heart of a spiritual man is a receiver. A receiver is an apparatus for receiving and changing an electrical signal into an audible or visible effect. (Revelation 4:5, "And out of the throne proceeded lightnings.").

2. The spiritual man is as a natural man using a radio. 1 Timothy 4:1 says, "Now the Spirit speaketh expressly (or definitely, clearly)."

3. The spiritual man is as a natural man using a computer. John 14:26 says, "He (the Holy Spirit) shall...bring all things to your remembrance." And Luke 12:12 says "The Holy Spirit shall teach you in the same hour." A computer saves stored information and retrieves it.

4. The spiritual man is as a natural man using a telephone. 1 Corinthians 14:2, 3 says, "For he that

180

speaketh in an unknown tongue speaketh...unto God." And God "speaketh unto men to edification (improve or educate), and exhortation (warn or urge), and comfort."

5. The spiritual man is as a natural man using a telegraph. 1 Corinthians 14:14 says, "For if I pray in an unknown tongue, my spirit prayeth, but my understanding is unfruitful." When we pray in an unknown tongue, messages are exchanged in the spirit bypassing the enemy's battleground, the mind. A telegraph is an apparatus or system for transmitting messages over a distance by coded electric signals.

Psalm 78:41 tells us, "They limited the Holy one of Israel." Why would we want to limit God in our life? People have so many misconceptions concerning the Holy Spirit and its work in our lives. This book is written to dispel these misconceptions, in order to help people receive God's very best, and usher into The Church the latter day glory! Very simply put, God is practical and many things in the natural are a reflection of the spiritual. Certainly in this age of technology, with people in hot pursuit for better, faster, and more information every person needs to know exactly what the Holy Spirit does, so we can be as up to date spiritually as we are naturally. When we are filled with the Holy Spirit, we are as a natural house with power or electricity, the lights are on, we're cookin', and things are workin'! But if we are not filled with the Holy

Spirit then we are without power, and simply put, we are as a natural house without electricity, the lights are not on, we are not cookin', and nothing is workin'! Spiritually speaking, because of false teaching and a lack of Bible study and a seeking relationship with the Lord, most people's spiritual lives are as up to date as the 1700's, but it is the year 2012. Even though we are in an awesome age naturally, and people are surrounded by the vast difference in the 1700's and the times we live in, many are still walking by candlelight, pulling their plow with oxen, and counting on horse-drawn carriages. They realize that since they have accepted Jesus they have some light, oxen are better than planting by hand, and horses are better than walking, so they resist the Holy Spirit, that power that fills the house with light to overflowing, and takes them from the manual, laborious life to a new abundant way, and takes them from 20 mph in life to 120 mph. Zechariah 4:6 says, "Not by might, nor by power, but **by my Spirit**, saith the Lord of hosts."